Le Caprice

AA Gill

Recipes by **Mark Hix**
Photography by **Henry Bourne**

First published in Great Britain in 1999 by Hodder and Stoughton
A division of Hodder Headline PLC

British Library Cataloguing in Publication Data

ISBN 0 340 73838 3

Printed and Bound in Great Britain
by Butler & Tanner Ltd, Frome and London.

Design and Art Direction by Unlimited

Unlimited would like to thank Mary Agace, Solange Azagury-Partridge, Nicola Formby,
Pete King, Judy Kleinman, Susan Minot and Charlotte Skene-Catling for their help.

A special thanks to Core Digital, particularly Scott Williams and Allan Finnamore for all
the digital imaging.

Flowers by Robert Hornsby

Le Caprice

Hodder & Stoughton

Contents

Weights, Measures and Servings

All recipes serve eight unless otherwise stated and are written to metric. They can be converted successfully to imperial by using the following tables except the pastry recipes where only metric should be used. Do not combine metric and imperial.

Standards Liquid

1 tsp	=	5 ml
1 tbsp	=	15 ml
1 fl oz	=	30 ml
1 oz	=	0.35 l
1 pint	=	20 fl oz
1 litre	=	35 fl oz

Standards Solid

1 oz	=	30 g
1 lb	=	16 oz (480 g)
1 g	=	0.35 oz
1 kg	=	2.2 lb

Liquid Conversions

Metric	Imperial
15 ml	$1/3$ fl oz
20 ml	$2/3$ fl oz
30 ml	1 fl oz
50 ml	1 $2/3$ fl oz
60 ml	2 fl oz
90 ml	3 fl oz
100 ml	3 $1/3$ fl oz
150 ml	5 fl oz ($1/4$ pint)
200 ml	6 $2/3$ fl oz
250 ml	8 fl oz
300 ml	10 fl oz ($1/2$ pint)
500 ml	16 $2/3$ fl oz
600 ml	20 fl oz (1 pint)
1 litre	1 $3/4$ pints
4 litres	7 pints

Solid Weight Conversions

Metric	Imperial
5 g	$1/6$ oz
10 g	$1/3$ oz
15 g	$1/2$ oz
30 g	1 oz
50 g	1 $2/3$ oz
60 g	2 oz
90 g	3 oz
100 g	3 $1/3$ oz
150 g	5 oz
200 g	6 $2/3$ oz
250 g	8 $1/3$ oz
300 g	10 oz
400 g	13 oz
480 g	16 oz (1 lb)
500 g	16 $2/3$ oz

Oven Temperature Conversions

°C	Gas	°F
110	_	225
120	_	250
140	1	275
150	2	300
160	3	325
175	4	350
190	5	375
200	6	400
220	7	425
230	8	450
240	9	475
260	10	500

Recipes

Soups & Stocks

Brunch

Starters

Main Courses

Vegetables

Desserts

Cocktails

Le Caprice

Swing through the revolving doors of Le Caprice and you know you are in a modern restaurant. In the eternal tug-of-war between the old world and the new, this sways towards the new. Its essence is American. New York, East Coast rather than California. It wears the perennial uniform of the twentieth century, black and white: the binary extremes of our time, the non-colour colours of ying and yang, truth and lies, newsprint, dress – formal and business, our world, the third world. The little come-and-go, anywhere, any time, smart and syncopated tones of the way we are now. Black and white picked out in the walls, in high contrast Bailey photographs.

There are a hundred and one signals that tell you what a restaurant expects of you and what you, in turn, can order from it. These photographs at Le Caprice are their cultural, political style statement. They are a time set in emulsion. All portraits, icons of a time that is ours and contemporary but already gone. The late 1960s, early '70s, Beaton with Nureyev, Muggeridge, Man Ray, an enigmatic Catherine Deneuve, Roman Polanski with a naked Sharon Tate, Fellini and Houston. They are faces that glare confidently out at you but whose names almost escape. Familiar, but they've somehow slipped into the gutter of Sunday magazines and celebrity profiles. It's a mild shock to realise how many of them are actually dead and, if not actually buried, well past their cultural sell-by dates. Still they pose on the periphery, in black and white.

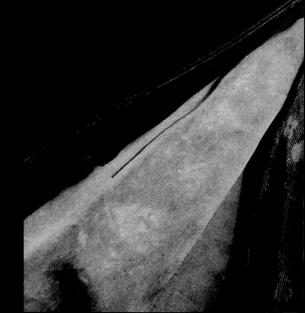

Marianne Faithfull, September 1964 by **David Bailey**

The least of these images is that they are arresting pictures; more importantly they set out Le Caprice's credentials, arty, liberal, intellectual, cosmopolitan, witty, gossipy and transient. The restaurant will always be here but the people who pass through it maybe won't. These pictures, like the cave paintings in the first smoky dining rooms, are a wish list, an invocation of the sorts of people this room is meant to attract, and they are a small joke at the expense of the old duffers' clubs around the corner.

Under these studiedly self-confident, anti-establishment faces sit this generation's 'A' list. The photographs are their *memento mori.* Le Caprice subtly reminds its customers of the ephemeral nature of fame and achievement; the applause and the grins, the appreciation are caught under glass on the walls although it's doubtful if any of the diners recognise their own reflections in the glass. And that's as it should be. *Carpe diem,* savour your own day.

There are other signals to decipher. There is a bar, a long bar, set with cutlery and glasses and napery, and bar stools with backs. Important that. A bar stool with a back invites you to linger. It's a knife-and-fork bar, not a leaning with your elbows staring into a glass bar. This is a place to meet for a light lunch, for a business chat, not a maudlin set-'em-up-Joe bar, but that American hybrid of a refectory table and a cocktail lounge, and it tells you that this is a relaxed place where you won't be asked to wear a tie, where a girl can sit down on her own. Here is a place that knows the value of your day, you can eat and run, one course and go. Bars imply all sorts of things: flirtation, camaraderie, business bonding.

Opposite is a piano, a white piano. In the evening a chap with a loquacious left hand will stroke out show tunes and sassy atmosphere. The unsung lyrics and rhythm that pat your bottom.

Sharon Tate and Roman Polanski, January 1969 by **David Bailey**

Cecil Beaton and Rudolf Nureyev, January 1965 by **David Bailey**

Le Caprice

Minted Broad Bean Soup
with Crumbled Feta
5.50

Belgian Endive Salad with Pommery Mustard Dressing	5.75
Chilled Beetroot Soup with Creamed Horseradish	5.75
Caesar Salad	6.75
Plum Tomato and Basil Galette	6.75
Buffalo Mozzarella with Baked Aubergine and Capers	7.50
Crispy Duck with Watercress Salad	8.50
Mixed Oriental Hors d'Oeuvres	8.75
Roasted Italian Onions with San Daniele Ham	9.75
Griddled Scallops with Mousseline Potato	12.25
Dressed Cornish Crab with Landcress	13.50
Sautéed Foie Gras with Glazed Apples	14.75

Truffle - Studded
Roasted Capon
13.50

Eggs Benedict	5.75	10.75
Risotto with Zucchini and Pecorino	6.75	10.50
Steak Tartare	7.75	14.75
Risotto Nero	8.75	13.25
Fettucine with Langoustine Tails	15.75	23.50

Tagliatelle with Ceps
8.75

Cold Ox Tongue and Veal
with Baby Beetroots
and Balsamico
12.75

Herb-roasted Lambs' Kidneys with seared cauliflower	9.75
Salmon Fishcake on a bed of sautéed spinach with sorrel sauce	11.25
Chopped Steak Americain with sautéed onions and pommes allumettes	11.50
Breast of Corn Fed Chicken with purple sprouting broccoli, plum tomatoes and olive oil	12.25
Char-grilled Squid and Italian Bacon with rocket and pimento salsa	12.75
Mexican Griddled Chicken Salad with guacamole and piquillo peppers	12.75
Confit of Duck with truffled summer cabbage and lentils	14.50
Deep-fried Haddock with minted pea purée, chips and tartare sauce	14.75
Roast Fillet of Cod with italian barley and barolo sauce	15.25
Peppered Blue Fin Tuna with green tomato relish	15.75
Grilled Rabbit with Rosemary polenta and black olives	16.75
Char-grilled Sirloin Steak with deep-fried onions and herb butter	18.75
Fillet of Sea Bass with jerusalem artichoke mash	21.75

Baked Razor Clams
with Parsley & Garlic
8.50

Lobster Salad
with Crushed Potatoes
and Alsace Bacon
21.50

Green Herb Salad	3.25 / 4.50	Allumettes or Medium Cut Chips	3.00
Mixed Tomatoes and Basil	3.50 / 6.25	Parmesan Baked Marrow with Wild Garlic	4.75
Wild Rocket and Parmesan	3.75 / 6.75	Spinach; creamed, buttered or steamed	4.75

Cover Charge 1.50 at Table
Last Orders Midnight

Service Not Included
We ask smokers to show consideration for other diners

All Prices include VAT
Open Every Day

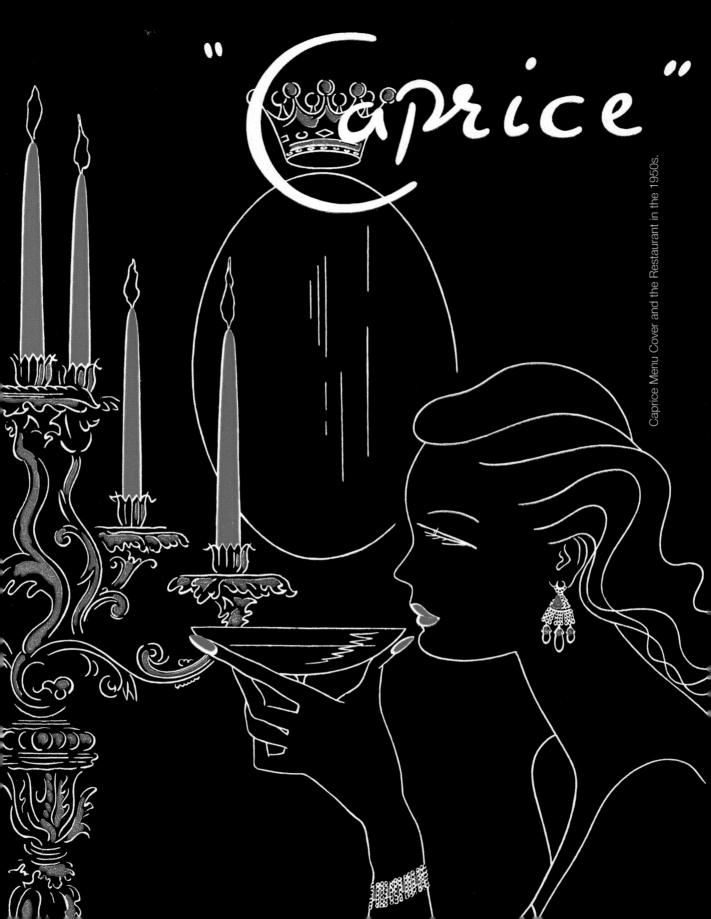

"*Caprice*"

The History

Mario Gallati opened The Caprice restaurant in 1947, not an auspicious time for eating out in London. Well, an even less auspicious time than the previous three hundred years. Rationing actually got tighter after the war, the country was near bankruptcy, there were shortages of everything – paper, cloth, bricks – the only glut was of holes in the ground but the war was over, the men were coming home and there was the first Labour government and a general sense of a new beginning, a sense of optimism. The Festival of Britain was being planned but still no restaurant could charge more than five bob for a meal, not that there was all that much to cook. The location, under a block of 1930s flats that Lord Beaverbrook lived in, had been a number of restaurants – The Corvette, Quintos and Cicogne, but until the Caprice, had never been a success. However, Mario Gallati, ex-*maître d'* of The Ivy, had no trouble finding backers for Caprice (no 'Le' in the original). Terence Rattigan, Ivor Novello and the famous agent A.D. Peters all put in money as did the Lord Mayor of London and the divinely named Viscountess Rhondda.

Mario Gallati deserves a footnote in this story. An Italian immigrant, he arrived in Britain after the First World War and was obviously a born restaurant manager, a true flunky with an inexhaustible appetite for snobbery and flattery. Through his years at The Ivy he had built up a loyal clientele in the theatre, cinema, publishing and newspapers and the sort of itinerant deposed royalty that had settled finally in London. Those who remember the old Caprice always mention the singular decoration, plush banquettes and ruched pink silk covering the walls. You couldn't get real silk of course so they used parachutes dyed in loganberry juice. The decorative *tour de force* was gold hands that stuck out of the walls holding fans. The Caprice was of an unsurpassed hideosity and an almost instant success. *Tout le monde* came to be fawned over and plan the brave new modern world. Gallati was already sixty when he started the Caprice and he finally retired at the end of the 1960s. The restaurant staggered on without him until 1975 when it was forced to close. With his legendary showbiz timing, Gallati died the same day. The restaurant had a couple of inconspicuous openings under new managements, culminating in the Arlington, a *faux* Edwardian clubbable place which folded in 1980 after only five months.

In 1981, Jeremy King and Chris Corbin came together respectively from the theatrical American restaurant Joe Allen and the highly successful French-ish restaurant Langan's Brasserie to take the lease. The mixture of Joe Allen and Langan's was central to the inspiration behind Le Caprice. It was to serve a range of food from well-made French brasserie dishes to quick and cheap American diner fare. It was to be a relaxed restaurant but with continental *savoir-faire*. Back then it was inspired. France and America are the two great locomotives of public dining and taking the best from each was exactly what London needed. That's not to say that Le Caprice was an instant success, indeed it came close to foundering. That's when you need to keep your nerve, when you're standing in an empty restaurant at 9.30 on a Thursday night. There was an evening, now firmly pressed into Le Caprice's mythology when Marie Helvin called to book a table and said she was going to bring Mick and Jerry *et al* and it would be rocking, wouldn't it? Chris and Jeremy called all their friends and told them to come and fill up the restaurant for free. They got people out of bed, people who'd already eaten. It worked, and the reputation began.

In the nineteen years during which Chris and Jeremy have run Le Caprice it must have influenced more restaurants in London than any other. Chefs and restaurateurs may not even realise just how many of the ideas and innovations in menus and service that have improved Britain's restaurants originated in Arlington Street. Ultimately, Le Caprice realised that waiting around for a bill, being coaxed with brandies and an unwanted sweet trolley was not what busy people wanted. They wanted to pay and get on. That was the thing about Le Caprice. It was invented as a restaurant for people who get on with life and if that sounds like a trite advertising slogan, well, it was created for copywriters too. Surprisingly, Le Caprice is not economically élitist; if you're running a restaurant where a good proportion of your regular clientele is theatrical or freelance, you must never forget to have cheap dishes on the menu for when they're not working. It is not on just to say 'hello' when they're in a West End run and buying champagne. They are customers for ever.

For nearly two decades, a table at Le Caprice has been the stock exchange of the arts and Chris and Jeremy and their managers have been its most successful brokers.

Vogue feature, 'A Kitchen Cinderella', December 1957, Snowdon. Jacqueline Chan and Tom Arnold

Soups

Stocks

Soups
and
Stocks

Soup

Back in the frosty dawn of post-rationing when I first went to restaurants, a starter meant soup. Soup or melon with either dried ginger or ham. Possibly a grapefruit half weirdly grilled with demerara sugar. But soup was the thing. It was more than likely cream of tomato, cream of mushroom, or mulligatawny if you were in the sort of place frequented by old Empire hands. And there was something else called Brown Windsor. Brown Windsor soup has a mythic status today. It's a sort of music-hall joke along with outside loos, washboards and Marcel waves.

It is actually impossible to find a recipe for Brown Windsor soup, once ubiquitous, now I doubt it's prepared from one year to the next. Generally it was an insipid, watery gravy with occasional shards of the unusable ends of parcel string in it. Occasionally it was powerfully noxious with thick lumps of motherless meat that would have disturbingly blancmange-pink centres. Brown Windsor sounded and tasted like the end of the Empire.

Soup as a genus nearly disappeared from menus. No other species of dish has been so affected by snobbery and fashion. It's now not unusual to find a menu without a single soup on it, and when they are there more often than not, they are Magimix frothy and banal. After plain roast meat, the oldest thing we cook, the original recipe, is soup. When you can make a thumb pot and you can boil water you can make soup. When you've made soup, Brown Windsor, the Empire and the Railway Hotel, Huddersfield, are only a few minor details and several thousand years away.

Soup has been the staple diet of working folk for most of our existence. Thick, lumpy, full of hidden treasures, quaggy with farinaceous beans. A sensuous mire of unwanted tops and tails, a tenderising bath for tough muscles and working sinews, slow cooked, generously flavoured and above all, cheap. For most of our existence, soup has been life in a dish, the one-stop lunch and dinner and still, if you ask for a litany of comfort food, soup will be in everybody's top ten.

It was really the French who took soup to a finishing school. Their shrugging and pouting classes who have so often appeared to have nothing better to do than make up rules for things that had previously worked perfectly well without rules decided, to the general discomfort of each other and the social insecurity of those below them, that soup was not a dish fit for lunch. How this arbitrary piece of social draconianism was arrived at no one is quite sure. Was there a secret convocation of hostesses and single gentlemen at Maxim's perhaps, who agreed to disseminate a fatwah on soup in the daytime? Was it the whim of a president's mistress who happened to have burnt her mouth on an impertinent marmite? Who knows. What we do know for sure is that soup was deemed *de trop* for lunch, precisely because it is so utterly perfect for lunch. This absurd rule is now three or four generations old, and nobody living has any idea why it ever existed, if they ever did, but there are still perfectly ordinary folk who are trusted with driving licences and bank accounts and the care of children but won't eat soup for lunch, simply won't.

Soup spoons, by the way, are those round specialist spoons that your gran told you to dip away from you and tip into your mouth – never suck, and always tilt the plate away. Soup spoons weren't invented until the 1920s, the Georgians and the Victorians used serving spoons. The invention of a specialist spoon was undoubtedly another reason for people to discard soup, that and the fact that you could buy the stuff in tins.

When meals dropped a course from four to three because of constraints of time, it was only natural that the elegant, hot but essentially vacuous soup should go. Soup came this close to being relegated to the cranky habitat of health food restaurants and old people's homes, and chicken soup – the Jewish penicillin. Its partial reprieve came from the oddest quarter, a place where the mores of fashion were quite unimpressed by French snobbery, where sucking, indeed slurping, was not frowned on but *de rigueur*. The fashion for Eastern food, particularly mongrelised with French or Italian dishes, made soup fashionable again. The Chinese, the Thais and Vietnamese have always held soup in high regard so restaurants found that if they could put coriander and lemongrass in it, people would eat it. The Chinese, by the way, eat their soup at the end of a meal, not at the beginning.

So soup still has a tenuous foothold on our menus, but old prejudices die hard. I remember being told not to order soup on Mondays because it was invariably made out of leftovers, and still some customers look at soup as being no more than a dustbin of bits. We have downgraded our oldest, most comforting and dependable dish, a friend who has stood by us in hard times and a complete meal, to a disposable course, to a sort of *amuse-gueule*.

If you look at Victorian cookbooks they are replete, resplendent with pages and pages and pages of soups, potages, bisques, marmites, chowders. There are oceans of soup still unmade and untasted. It was the Duchess of Windsor, her of the social-climbing-altitude record, who said that 'soup was a lake and no meal should start with a lake'. It's not even a proper aphorism.

Le Caprice goes some way to repaying the huge debt of gratitude we owe to the soup tureen. There are usually two or three soups, and for me they are the high point of the kitchen's art, because they take soup seriously and they make their own stocks. Some customers, who are now brave enough not to be dictated to by dead French hostesses and the Duchess of Windsor, even eat them for lunch.

The soups here are of the binary type, that is matched pairs of flavours: Creamed Cider and Onion; Butternut Squash and Ginger; Beetroot and Horseradish. They are both hot and cold. Do make the Broad Bean with Feta, it's simple and it's fulsome and someone had to finally do something with feta that didn't involve cucumber triangles and bouzouki music.

The soup I miss, the soup of childhood, is turtle. From those old railway hotels of badly typed menus and singed grapefruit, there was often turtle soup. Splendid, thin, fugitive and exactly what you would imagine a turtle to taste of, urbane, pedantic, somehow musty and scholarly. The waiter would bring a schooner of sherry. It was the perfect combination, exactly the savour of Oxford quads and dusty scholarship. A spoonful of turtle soup would whisk you back to the nineteenth century. The incomprehensible news vendors outside might have been shouting that the great redoubt at Sebastopol had finally been taken. Just because these great green tortoises are rare doesn't seem to me anything like good enough a reason for not making them into soup. They were born to be soup, they even come with their own tureen. There was always mock turtle soup made with a calf's head. More famous than the real thing thanks to Lewis Carroll. Le Caprice doesn't serve turtle or mock turtle, so there's no point in going on about them – and there's been far too much mocking of soup.

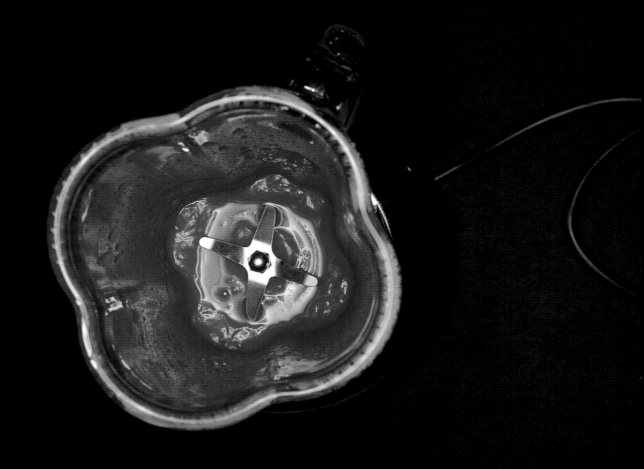

Chilled Beetroot Soup with Creamed Horseradish

1 small onion, peeled and roughly chopped

1 leek, trimmed, washed and roughly chopped

5 g thyme

30 ml vegetable oil

700-800 g cooked beetroot, roughly chopped

2 ltrs Vegetable Stock (see page 35)

salt and freshly ground black pepper

50 ml good-quality balsamic vinegar

to serve

60 g freshly grated horseradish or 100 g good-quality horseradish sauce

60 g crème fraîche

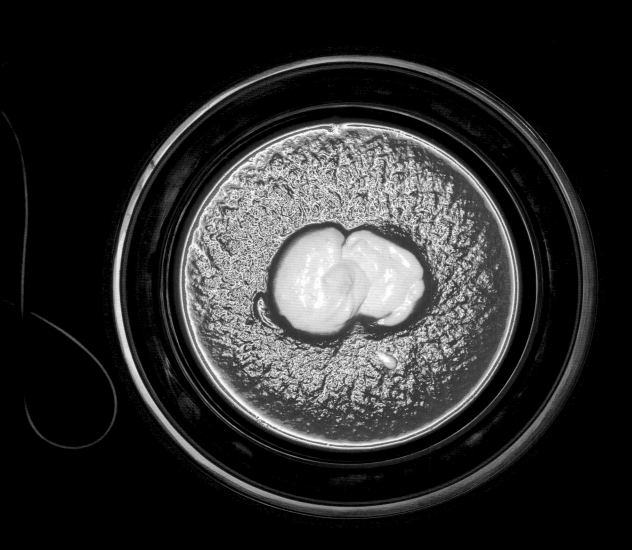

Sweat the onion, leek and thyme for a few minutes in the vegetable oil until they are soft.

Add the beetroot and the vegetable stock, bring to the boil, season to taste and simmer for 35-40 minutes.

Process in a blender until smooth, then strain through a fine-meshed sieve.

Allow the soup to cool, then refrigerate it for a few hours until it is well chilled, or if you're short of time, put into the freezer.

Once chilled, check and adjust seasoning and stir in the balsamic vinegar.

Mix the crème fraîche with the horseradish.

To serve, ladle the soup into bowls, and top with a spoonful of the creamed horseradish.

Minted **Broad Bean** Soup with Crumbled Feta

An interesting soup that can be served hot or cold in spring, summer or autumn.

1 medium onion, peeled and roughly chopped

2 leeks, trimmed, washed and roughly chopped

5 g thyme

30 ml olive oil

1 tbsp plain flour

1 ltr Vegetable Stock (see page 35)

750g podded fresh (1.5–2 kg) or frozen broad beans

salt and freshly ground white pepper

to serve

4 large ripe tomatoes, peeled and seeded

5 g mint, leaves only, chopped

5 g coriander leaves, chopped

30 ml extra-virgin olive oil

salt and freshly ground black pepper

150 g good-quality Greek feta, crumbled

Gently cook the onion, leek and thyme in the olive oil, without colouring, until soft.

Add the flour, stir well, then gradually add the vegetable stock.

Bring to the boil, add the broad beans, season with salt and pepper then simmer for 15 minutes.

Process the soup in a blender until smooth, then strain through a fine-meshed sieve, and return the soup to a clean saucepan.

Meanwhile, finely dice the tomato flesh and mix it with the mint, coriander and olive oil, then season with salt and pepper.

Reheat the soup, or serve it cold, then spoon the tomato relish on top with some crumbled feta.

Cumin Spiced **Parsnip** Soup

60 g butter

1 medium onion, peeled and roughly chopped

1 leek, trimmed, washed and roughly chopped

1 kg parsnips, peeled and roughly chopped

2 tsps ground cumin

1 clove garlic, peeled and crushed

40 g root ginger, scraped and finely chopped

5 g thyme

3 ltrs Vegetable Stock (see page 35)

salt and freshly ground white pepper

60 ml double cream

10 g coriander, finely chopped

Melt the butter in a large, thick-bottomed pan and gently cook the onion, leek and parsnips until soft.

Add the cumin, garlic, ginger and thyme and cook for a further 2–3 minutes.

Pour in the stock, bring to the boil, season with salt and pepper and simmer for 30 minutes.

Process the soup in a blender, and strain it through a sieve.

Return it to a clean pan, pour in the cream, stir in the coriander and correct the seasoning, if necessary.

If the soup is too thick, add a little more stock or water.

Butternut Squash and Ginger Soup

1 leek, trimmed, washed and roughly chopped

1 onion, peeled and roughly chopped

2 carrots, peeled and roughly chopped

50 g root ginger, scraped and finely chopped

5 g thyme

1/2 small chilli, seeded and roughly chopped

30 ml vegetable oil, plus a little extra

1 kg butternut squash, peeled, seeded and roughly chopped

1.5 ltrs Vegetable Stock (see page 35)

salt and freshly ground black pepper

60 g pumpkin seeds

Gently cook the leek, onion, carrots, ginger, thyme and chilli in the vegetable oil until soft, then add the butternut squash and vegetable stock and bring to the boil.

Season with salt and pepper then simmer for 20 minutes.

Process the soup in a blender until smooth, then strain through a fine-meshed sieve.

Lightly brown the pumpkin seeds in a little vegetable oil in a frying-pan, season with salt and pepper, and drain on some kitchen paper.

Reheat the soup and adjust the consistency with a little vegetable stock or water, if necessary, and check the seasoning.

Serve with the pumpkin seeds scattered on top.

Creamed **Cider** and **Onion** Soup

10 medium onions, peeled and thinly sliced

10 g thyme, leaves removed and chopped

30 ml vegetable oil

60 g butter

50 g flour

100 ml dry cider

2 ltrs Vegetable Stock (see page 35)

salt and freshly ground black pepper

100 ml double cream

In a thick-bottomed pan with a lid on, gently cook the onions and thyme, without colouring, in the vegetable oil until soft.

Add the butter and continue to cook for a few minutes. Add the flour and stir on a low heat for another minute or so.

Slowly add the cider, stirring constantly, then gradually add the vegetable stock. Bring to the boil and simmer for 1 hour.

Half-way through cooking it may be necessary to add some water if the soup is becoming too thick, and adjust the seasoning.

Finally add the cream, bring the soup back to the boil and serve.

Fish Stock

Butternut Squash and Ginger Soup

Stocks

In the kitchen at Le Caprice 50 kilos of veal, chicken and fish bones arrive daily to make stocks for sauces and soups. At home it is useful to keep some concentrated stocks in the freezer. If you need 1 litre it takes no longer to make 5 litres, and concentrate what you don't use. Freeze it in little tubs; when you need it defrost it and add water.

Here are four simple stocks that you will need for recipes throughout the book. The quantities given for each provide 5 litres. If ordering the bones in advance from your butcher ask him to chop them up for you: you will get more bones in your pot and thus more flavour.

Dark **Meat** Stock

2 kg beef, veal, lamb or chicken bones, chopped

3 medium onions, peeled and chopped

5 medium carrots, peeled and chopped

1 small head celery, chopped

2 leeks, trimmed, washed and chopped

1/2 head garlic, peeled and chopped

50 g tomato purée

20 black peppercorns

10 g thyme

1 bay leaf

Pre-heat the oven to 200°C/gas mark 6.

Roast the bones and the vegetables for 15-20 minutes until lightly coloured, giving them a good turn every so often.

When everything is a nice golden brown, add the tomato purée and stir well.

Return the pan to the oven for another 10 minutes.

Then put the bones and vegetables into a large pot, cover them with water and add the rest of the ingredients.

Bring to the boil, skim off any scum that forms and simmer for 3–4 hours.

The stock will need topping up occasionally with water to keep the ingredients covered, and skimming.

Strain it through a fine-meshed sieve and remove any fat with a ladle.

Check the strength of the stock and reduce it if necessary.

Chicken Stock

2 kg chicken bones, chopped

3 medium leeks, trimmed, washed and chopped

3 medium onions, chopped

1 small head celery, chopped

10 g thyme

1 bay leaf

20 black peppercorns

Wash the chicken bones to remove any blood.

Put them into a pot with the rest of the ingredients and cover everything with cold water.

Bring to the boil, skim off any scum that forms, and simmer for 2 hours.

It may need topping up occasionally with water to keep the ingredients covered, and skimming.

Strain it through a fine-meshed sieve and remove any fat with a ladle.

Check the strength of the stock and reduce it if necessary.

Vegetable Stock

3 medium onions, peeled and chopped

1 small head celery, chopped

3 leeks, trimmed, washed and chopped

5 medium carrots, peeled and chopped

2 bay leaves

5 g thyme

20 black peppercorns

a handful parsley

1 tsp fennel seeds

Put all the ingredients into a pot and cover them with cold water.

Bring it to the boil, skim off any scum that forms and simmer for 30–40 minutes.

Strain it through a fine-meshed sieve. Check the strength of the stock and reduce it if necessary.

Fish Stock

2 kg white fish bones, sole, trout, brill, etc.

2 medium leeks, trimmed, washed and chopped

2 medium onions, peeled and chopped

1/2 head celery, chopped

1/2 lemon

1 tsp fennel seeds

20 black peppercorns

5 g thyme

1 bay leaf

parsley or parsley stalks

Wash the bones in cold water.

Put them into a pot with the rest of the ingredients, cover with cold water and bring to the boil, skim off any scum that forms and simmer for 20 minutes, skimming occasionally.

Strain it through a fine-meshed sieve. Check the strength of the stock and reduce it if necessary.

Brunch

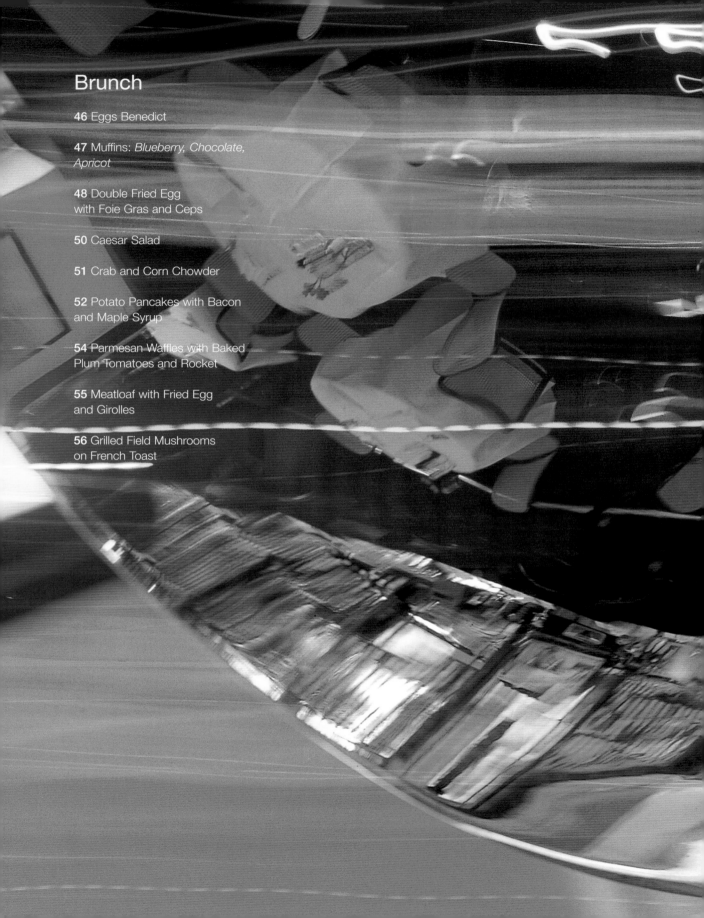

Brunch

'The single greatest invention of the twentieth century?
Easy. There is no contest.
Eggs Benedict.'

The single greatest invention of the twentieth century? Easy. There is no contest. Eggs Benedict.

Leave aside the fact that it's a fantastic combination of ingredients, someone somewhere, a true hero of the century said:

'Eggs and bacon are a marriage made in heaven's kitchen. They are unimprovable, so I will improve them.' From such hubris, genius is born.

Add an English muffin. (Why English? Has anyone ever seen a German muffin or even a Nicaraguan one?) And hollandaise sauce, which is a tricky balancing act. Do I want hollandaise on an egg? A rich butter sauce with added egg yolk?
Yes. Eureka!

The heavenly quartet of complementary flavours and textures and Le Caprice serves the very best. Eggs Benedict is the golden symbol of modernity. It's what is known at Le Caprice as an attitude dish. You see it on the menu and it comes with associations and assumptions, it's relaxed, it's sybaritic.

What the hamburger is to mass eating, Eggs Benedict is to the middle classes. It's a Big Mac who's read Proust.

Actually, they've quite a lot in common. Apart from the bun, they are essentially constructions rather than cuisine, they can be made by short-order cooks, although not necessarily well, and they both have that up-front uncomplicated but deeply attractive flavour that is a million tastebuds away from the sly civility and courtly deception of *haute cuisine* cookery.

Eggs Benedict is as direct as an advertising punch line, it is a dish that says something about you and the person you want to be. Eggs Benedict is a people person, it's dressed down, it's loafers and a polo shirt, it's unisex cologne, it's Sunday papers and films with subtitles and baby papooses. It's sybaritic without being self-indulgent. It's that smooth, smart, committed liberal, sexy, witty, off-white, lifestyle thing, that PR agencies and glossy magazines have been teasing us with for a generation. It's modern – your grandfather never ate Eggs Benedict. It's you and it's me and it's the whole shtick of post-war, post-modern, politically savvy, free-market, free-thinking, free-from-want, free-as-a-bird, happy-ever-after, Western capitalist dream, and which of us in the goddamn world doesn't want that? Eggs Benedict is an on-the-plate, runny, gloopy, sentimental, mouth-coating revelation. Reading 'Eggs Benedict' on a menu is politically and socially potent and pregnant with meaning – the clenched fist, or perhaps the 'High Five' manifesto of nice people.

Now, you may be thinking this is all well over the top. Well, wake up and smell the coffee, because Eggs Benedict is the standard bearer, the heart and soul of brunch, and brunch, well, brunch is us. **That rarest phenomenon of the millennium, a new meal.**

If I were the wicked king in a fairy story where some lovelorn prince wanted to marry my daughter and I had to set him impossible tasks, you can forget the golden apple and all the dragon's teeth nonsense, I'd ask him to invent a new meal. Brunch is the only one this century.

Although it is American in origin, brunch is an international meal, with elements plundered from around the world, German, Jewish, French, Italian, British. Foodies go on about fusion food, world food, binary Esperanto international air miles food, but we never think about brunch, a happy synthesis of pan-glottal togetherness, an edible Benetton advertisement.

The daily milestones of breakfast, lunch and dinner are fixed in our biology, set in porcelain and silver and more indelibly set in gut and appetite. The times of our meals have changed only to follow the sun. We are no longer daylight slaves, and meals have become shorter and smaller, because we don't need to take in so many calories. Central heating and less physically demanding work allow us to make light of meals.

And meals have got shorter simply because we've got other things to do. More entertaining things to do than sit around and watch each other eat, and gossip about the fifteen people we all know in common and moan that they haven't invented television or movies yet.

We can still wonder in consternation at the dinners eaten by the Georgians, meals that went on for eight or nine courses, maybe even twenty or twenty-five courses, and it's no wonder that people like Dr Johnson were famous in their lifetimes as much for their spoken words as their written. Trying to eat that much was a Herculean task, but trying to make polite, witty conversation for six hours straight was positively Sisyphean.

Although the main meals of our days have remained, we have sadly lost a depressing number of small peripheral food stops, little meals that couldn't adapt to mankind, that have been swept away by modern life. Far sadder and more poignant than the extinction of some unremarkable, furry marsupial with dubious personal habits or some fetid, rank piece of swamp, the near extinction of elevenses is not mourned by any right-on pressure group and who now weep for the pre-breakfast breakfast, the small solitary, meditative meal of tea and biscuits (cheese and pickled herring if you're a German) that was eaten in your bedroom before breakfast proper was approached. Dinner has encroached on to the territory once vouchsafed for supper, which cheesily gambolled and basked in pickle, but the saddest, most poignant absence must be for high tea, that Sumatran rhino of comestibles, a wonderful down-to-earth repast of breaded ham and salad or meat pies, bread and butter, tea cakes, fruit tarts and copious cups of tea, served immediately the working day had finished. It was a ravenous man's meal, but now most of us need to eat less and we can hold on until eight.

But we have invented brunch, a horrid name but fabulous company. Brunch was an inspired idea. Modern breakfast has become medicinal, the consumption of a bowl of food or vitamins or hangover cures, breakfast is a hit-and-run, self-administrated pharmacy of bowel food, and lunch is too far away from waking, and it's too much of a performance, heavy with the gout of workaday appointments, so brunch really only exists at weekends, and truly only on Sundays. It's a meal that has to be taken in a relaxed way, it's as celebratory as Christmas dinner, or Lenten pancakes. Brunch is the celebration of leisure time, it's an unconstructed Armani meal, as long or as short as you wish with as many courses. It includes both fruit juice and alcohol and coffee. It's eating canapés and puddings. Brunch is taken with just a fork in your fingers, it's a meal that you can take the kids to without excuse or apology, you can read the papers. There are no rules for brunch, no snobbery, no etiquette, just mild desires, a static grazing and most importantly of all, it's relaxed. Relaxed is the most evocative word of the late twentieth century. Preface anything with the word relaxed and we sit up and beg for it.

The crowd on Sundays at Le Caprice is quite different from the rest of the week. They look over the complementary Sunday supplements as if they were family photo albums. The kiddies (fresh from their packaging of a top-range Volvo) happily scribble with the thoughtfully provided wax crayons.

This, for a couple of hours, is a secular service of thanksgiving, a cathedral to the loveliness of us, a heartfelt prayer, a thank-you for low interest credit and wet wipes, thank you for Larry Sanders and Martin Amis, thank you for Cutler and Gross sunglasses and Joseph T-shirts, thank you for the Alternative Investment Market, thank you for Kiehl's moisturiser and e-mail, thank you for Nelson Mandela and de-caff cappuccino.

So here are the recipes for brunch. Make them if you can. I've yet to experience a perfect brunch on a plate, in a private kitchen. It always ends up just being a cooked breakfast served late, and that's not the thing at all. Cooked breakfast is what your parents had, cooked breakfast is, well, mahogany sideboards and old English thick-cut. It's kippers and that's not what you or your Eggs Benedict are all about at all. A piece of advice though, it's not in the recipe, but if you want to make brunch, it's best to add a great big spoonful of relax.

for the hollandaise sauce

70 ml white wine vinegar

80 ml water

2 small shallots, peeled and chopped

a few sprigs tarragon

1 bay leaf

10 black peppercorns

400 g unsalted butter

5 medium egg yolks

salt and freshly ground white pepper

to serve

8 slices Kasseler ham or sweet-cured back bacon

4 muffins

8 eggs, size 3

400 g hollandaise sauce

Eggs Benedict

To make the hollandaise sauce: place the vinegar, water, shallots, herbs and peppercorns in a saucepan and reduce the liquid to about a tablespoonful.

Strain and put aside.

Melt the butter and simmer it for 5–10 minutes.

Take off the heat, leave to cool a little, then pour off the pure fat where it has separated from the whey and discard the whey.

This helps to keep the sauce thick.

Put the egg yolks into a small stainless-steel bowl with half of the vinegar reduction and whisk over a pan of gently simmering water until the mixture begins to thicken and become frothy.

Slowly trickle in the butter, whisking continuously – an electric hand whisk will help. If the butter is added too quickly the sauce will separate.

When you have added two-thirds of the butter, taste the sauce and add a little more or all of the reduction.

Then put in the rest of the butter.

The sauce should not be too vinegary: the vinegar should just cut the oiliness of the butter.

Season with salt and pepper, cover with clingfilm and leave in a warm, not hot, place until needed.

The sauce can be reheated over a bowl of hot water and lightly whisked again.

To serve, grill the bacon, lightly toast the muffins and soft-poach the eggs.

Place the bacon on the muffin with the poached egg on top and coat it with a couple of generous spoonfuls of the hollandaise.

Blueberry Muffins

Makes approximately 16 muffins.

220 g unsalted butter

110 g caster sugar

20 g honey

3 medium eggs, beaten

260 g plain flour

20 g baking powder

150 ml milk

250 g frozen or fresh blueberries

Pre-heat the oven to 175°C/gas mark 4.

In a food-mixer, cream together the butter, sugar and honey until light and fluffy. Turn down the speed, add the eggs and mix well.

Sift the flour and baking powder together, then fold carefully but thoroughly into the butter mixture. Stir in the milk, a little at a time.

Add the blueberries and stir well until the mixture begins to turn blue.

Spoon the batter into greased muffin or 5–6-cm cake tins and bake for 15–20 minutes.

They are done if they feel springy when you prod them with a finger.

Chocolate Muffins

Makes approximately 16 muffins.

110 g unsalted butter

220 g caster sugar

20 g honey

2 eggs

180 g plain flour

20 g baking power

80 g cocoa

170 ml milk

50 g dark chocolate buttons

Pre-heat the oven to 175°C/gas mark 4.

In a food-mixer, cream together the butter, sugar and honey until light and fluffy. Turn down the speed, add the eggs and mix well.

Sift the flour, baking powder and cocoa together, then fold carefully but thoroughly into the butter mixture.

Stir in the milk, a little at a time. Add the chocolate buttons and mix well.

Spoon the mixture into greased muffin or 5–6-cm cake tins and bake for 15–20 minutes. They are done if they feel springy when you prod them with a finger.

Apricot Muffins

Makes approximately 16 muffins.

110 g unsalted butter

220 g caster sugar

20 g honey

2 eggs

260 g plain flour

20 g baking powder

200 ml milk

100 g dried apricots, soaked in cold water overnight and chopped

Pre-heat the oven to 175°C/gas mark 4.

In a food-mixer, cream to-gether the butter, sugar and honey until light and fluffy. Turn down the speed, add the eggs and mix well.

Sift together the flour and baking powder then fold carefully but thoroughly into the butter mix. Add the apricots and mix well. Stir in the milk, a little at a time.

Spoon the mixture into greased muffin or 5–6-cm cake tins and bake for 15–20 minutes. They are done if they feel springy when you prod them with a finger.

When you're lucky enough to find someone who stocks fresh foie gras (not pâte de foie gras), you will more than likely have to buy a whole lobe.

Usually you will need to order it in advance from your local butcher or deli.

1 lobe fresh duck or goose foie gras (approx. 500–800 g)

500–600 g fresh ceps

75 ml extra-virgin olive oil

salt and pepper

16 medium eggs, plus extra for breakages

60 g butter

5 g parsley, finely chopped

Double-Fried Egg with Foie Gras and Ceps

Take a sharp knife and a large jug filled with hot water. Dip the knife into the hot water then cut the foie gras at a slight angle into $1^1/_2$ - 2 cm thick slices. Put them into the fridge until required.

If the ceps look very sandy or dirty, scrape them with a small knife and wash them briefly in a bowl of water, then dry them on a cloth.

Slice them through, not too thinly, then heat a heavy frying-pan until it is almost smoking.

Add a little olive oil, then the ceps a couple of handfuls at a time.

Lightly season them and stir them every so often until they are nicely coloured.

Then drain them in a colander or on a tray lined with some kitchen paper.

You will need 4 ramekins or cups, each big enough to hold 2 eggs.

Carefully crack an egg white into each pot, then drop in the yolk.

With the second egg, put in only the yolk. (You can freeze the whites for another time.)

This may seem a little tedious but separating the first egg breaks down the albumen a little so that when the second yolk is dropped in it sits in the white nicely when it is cooked.

Heat a heavy frying-pan again, until it is almost smoking.

Turn down the heat and lightly season the foie gras with salt and pepper, then fry without any oil for a minute on each side.

Don't be alarmed at the amount of fat that comes out of the liver when cooking!

Drain the foie gras on some kitchen paper. Lightly oil a couple of preferably non-stick frying-pans, heat them gently, then drop in the double eggs.

Once they begin to set, place a slice of foie gras in the egg white and continue to cook, keeping the egg soft.

Meanwhile reheat the ceps in a pan with butter and the parsley.

To serve, slide the eggs on to warm plates and spoon over the ceps.

300 ml of good
mayonnaise

juice of 1 lemon

4 garlic cloves, peeled
and crushed

16 anchovy fillets

50 ml olive oil,
mixed with 50 ml
vegetable oil

4 garlic cloves,
peeled and halved

5 slices thick white
bread, crust removed
and cut into 1-cm cubes

salt and freshly ground
black pepper

50 g Parmesan cheese,
grated

1 iceberg lettuce,
washed and dried

2 firm, crisp Cos
or Romaine lettuces,
washed and dried

Caesar Salad

Put the mayonnaise,
lemon juice, crushed
garlic and eight anchovy
fillets in the blender,
process until smooth
and pour the mixture
into a bowl.

Chop the remaining
anchovy fillets and fold
them into the sauce.

If it is too thick to pour
easily thin it with a
little water.

Gently heat the oil
slowly with the halved
garlic cloves.

Fry the bread cubes
until they are golden,
then drain them on
kitchen paper.

Season, and sprinkle
with a little Parmesan
while they are still warm.

Tear the lettuces into
pieces and put them
in a bowl.

Toss them with the
dressing and the rest of
the Parmesan.

Scatter the croutons
on top and serve
immediately.

for the base

30 g butter

1 small onion, peeled and finely chopped

1 clove garlic, peeled and crushed

100 g canned sweetcorn kernels

1/2 small red pepper, seeded and roughly chopped

1 small chilli, seeded and chopped

1 tsp tomato purée

1.5 ltrs Vegetable Stock (see page 35)

90 g fresh brown crabmeat

salt and freshly ground black pepper

for the garnish

30 g butter

1 small onion, peeled and finely chopped

1/2 small red pepper, seeded and finely chopped

1 medium potato, peeled and cut into 1/2 -cm dice

100 g canned sweetcorn kernels

250 ml Vegetable Stock

5 g parsley, washed and finely chopped

60 ml double cream

90 g freshly picked white crabmeat

salt and freshly ground black pepper

Crab and Corn **Chowder**

To make the soup base, melt the butter in a medium-sized thick-bottomed pan and gently cook the onion, garlic, sweetcorn, pepper and chilli until soft.

Add the tomato purée, vegetable stock and brown crabmeat, then bring to the boil and season with salt and pepper.

Simmer for 45–50 minutes, then process in a jug blender and strain through a sieve. Put to one side.

For the garnish melt the butter in a small pan and gently cook the onion and red pepper until soft.

Add the potato, sweetcorn and vegetable stock, bring to the boil and simmer for about 10 minutes until the potato is just cooked.

Add the garnish to the base, with the parsley, double cream and white crabmeat. Bring back to the boil and season with salt and pepper if necessary.

If the soup is a little too thick, add some more vegetable stock.

1 small potato, peeled, cooked, mashed and cooled

1 medium egg, separated

50 g plain flour

50 g potato flour (optional: replace with ordinary flour if unavailable)

100 ml milk

salt and freshly ground black pepper

a pinch of freshly ground nutmeg

vegetable oil for frying

to serve

16 rashers sweetcure bacon or Kasseler ham

100 ml maple syrup

Potato **Pancakes** with Bacon and Maple Syrup

Put the mashed potato into a mixing bowl with the egg yolk and both of the flours.

Whisk to form a smooth paste by adding a little of the milk at a time.

Season with salt, pepper and nutmeg.

Whisk the egg white until stiff then fold into the mix.

Rub a little oil over the base of a non-stick, or your favourite, pancake pan then gently heat it.

Pour an eighth of the mixture into the pan, not letting it spread too much: the pancakes should be fairly thick.

Cook for 30–40 seconds on each side, carefully turning with a spatula.

Continue with the rest of the mixture.

The pancakes can be put directly on to the serving dish then reheated in a moderately hot oven or under the grill just before serving.

Meanwhile lightly grill the bacon and serve it on the pancakes with a generous pouring of maple syrup.

Start to make this dish the day before as the tomatoes will need to be semi-dried overnight in the oven.

16 plum tomatoes, quartered

5 g thyme, leaves removed and chopped

fine crystal sea salt

250–300 g rocket

10 ml Balsamic Dressing (see page 71)

90 g Parmesan cheese (whole piece)

for the waffles

220 g plain flour

1/2 tsp baking powder

3 eggs, beaten

500 ml milk

100 g Cheddar, grated

100 g freshly grated Parmesan

5 g chives, finely chopped

5 g parsley, finely chopped

salt and freshly ground black pepper

Parmesan **Waffles** with Baked Plum Tomatoes and Rocket

Pre-heat the oven to 110°C/gas mark 1/4.

Lay the tomatoes on a baking-tray and scatter over the chopped thyme.

Season lightly with sea salt.

Leave in the oven overnight (at least 10 hours) to dry out, after which they should have reduced in size by half.

To make the waffles, mix together the flour, baking powder and eggs, then slowly whisk in the milk.

Add the two cheeses and the herbs, then season with salt and pepper.

Pre-heat a waffle machine and lightly rub it with oil.

Cook the waffles for 2–3 minutes (they can be crisped up in the oven before serving).

To serve, put the warm waffles on a plate.

Toss the rocket with the balsamic dressing and the dried tomatoes then arrange it in a pile in the middle of each waffle.

Shave the Parmesan over the rocket with a vegetable peeler.

for the meatloaf

2 medium onions, peeled and finely chopped

2 cloves garlic, peeled and crushed

10 g thyme, leaves removed and chopped

30 ml vegetable oil

300 g coarsely minced fatty pork

300 g coarsely minced beef

150 g fresh white breadcrumbs

5 tbsps Worcestershire sauce

5 tsps Dijon mustard

2 tsps celery salt

salt and freshly ground black pepper

to serve

400–500 g girolle mushrooms (or an alternative if not available)

olive or vegetable oil for frying

60 g butter

1 clove garlic, peeled and crushed

salt and freshly ground black pepper

10 g parsley, washed and finely chopped

flour for dusting

Meatloaf with Fried Egg and Girolles

Pre-heat the oven to 190°C/gas mark 5.

Gently cook the onion, garlic and thyme in the vegetable oil for a few minutes until soft.

Transfer into a bowl and leave to cool.

Mix the minced pork, beef and breadcrumbs with the onion mixture, then add the Worcestershire sauce, Dijon mustard, celery salt and season well with salt and pepper.

Test the mixture by making a little flat cake and frying it.

Taste and adjust the seasoning, adding more Worcestershire sauce if needed.

Press the mixture into a loaf tin or a large terrine mould, then cover the top with tin foil.

Put it into a deep roasting-tin containing about 4 cm of hot water as a bain-marie, then place on the middle shelf of the oven and cook for 50–60 minutes.

Test the meatloaf by inserting a thin knife or roasting fork in the centre: if it's hot in the middle it's cooked.

Remove the tin from the bain-marie, then leave it to cool. Refrigerate for a few hours until cold and it has set.

Avoid washing the girolles unless they are particularly dirty when you should clean them in a bowl of water, then drain and dry them on kitchen paper.

Heat a little olive oil in a heavy frying-pan and cook them a few at a time on a high heat for 2–3 minutes.

Add the butter and the crushed garlic, season with salt and pepper and

continue to cook for a minute or so.

Finally, add the chopped parsley, remove from the heat and keep warm.

Remove the meatloaf from the tin and cut it into 1 1/2 -cm slices.

Lightly flour them and fry in a little vegetable oil for a couple of minutes on each side until golden, then keep warm.

Lightly fry the eggs in some olive or vegetable oil, and serve 1 on each slice of meatloaf, scattered with the girolles.

8 medium onions,
peeled and thinly sliced

5 g thyme, leaves
removed and chopped

100 ml vegetable oil

salt and freshly ground
black pepper

100 g butter

16 thin slices of white
bread, crusts removed

500–600 g medium-
sized field mushrooms

3 eggs, beaten

Grilled
Field
Mushrooms
on
French
Toast

Gently cook the onions and thyme in a covered pan in 30 ml of the vegetable oil until soft.

Season with salt and pepper, add 50 g of the butter and continue to cook without the lid until the onions begin to colour.

Remove from the heat and leave to cool.

Divide the onions between 8 slices of the bread, then press the other slices firmly on top to make 8 sandwiches.

Pre-heat a grill as hot as it will go, season the mushrooms and cook for about 5 minutes on each side adding the other 50 g of butter half-way through cooking.

Heat the rest of the vegetable oil in a frying pan, dip the sandwiches in the beaten eggs and fry for 2–3 minutes on each side until golden.

Serve with the grilled mushrooms on the French toasts.

Restaurants

Over ten thousand years of human culture, the concept of having a special building or room to eat in is very recent, only about two hundred years old. After you've fixed everything else, the nuts and bolts that go into making a functioning culture, plumbing, power, heat and light, trade, leisure time, roads, transport, a system of laws and policing, then and only then, can you relax and think about eating out.

Oh, and you must have a democracy. Restaurants only really work with democracy. It's a truth you don't often see on a menu. The birth of restaurants as we know them came with the French Revolution; along with food, a restaurant serves freedom of speech and association, which is why they have never done particularly well in countries that don't like people who speak to each other and meet in groups.

Dining out is, if not the greatest gift of the Age of Reason and the Rights of Man and all that *égalité*, *fraternité* and *liberté* stuff, then certainly its most popular one. Every time you are handed a menu you should say a quiet thank-you to Messrs Danton, Lafayette and Voltaire. By cutting off the heads of all the people who employed cooks, the revolutionary French managed, at a stroke as it were, to invent a new trade – public chef. The cooks of the aristocracy became the chefs of taverns and hotels, and French *haute cuisine* went public and middle class.

True to their origins, restaurants are still the places to foment the small revolutions of your life: to acquire a mistress; dump a wife; celebrate a promotion; pitch a deal. The Frenchness of eating out has been replicated round the world, not just in French food and cooking, but in menus written in French and the French version of interior design.

If we have the French to thank for the invention of restaurants, then making them fun is down to the Americans. It was the French, for all their *égalité* stuff, who imbued public dining with all the copious hierarchical snobbery and exclusive etiquette that it could manage. It was the Americans, at the start of this century, who loosened their collars, rolled up their sleeves and decided that restaurants were about other stuff but mostly they were about fun, and to have fun you have to be relaxed.

The two overriding cultural influences on restaurants are the oil of America and the vinegar of France. A property of each is that they don't like to mix and need to be copiously shaken. Together they give you comfort and elegance but like the two ends of civilisation's see-saw, restaurants tilt from one to the other as fashion dictates, but all restaurants need them both.

'If we are what we eat, shouldn't we be eating people?'

Someone sent me that on a cartoon, a derivative of Roy Lichtenstein's stylish woman looking cool and aggressive.

It's a take on the most misunderstood and misquoted aphorism about food.

'Tell me what you eat and I'll tell you who you are.'

Brillat Savarin, a refugee, snob, intellectual, towering Epicurean glutton and, incidentally, the Abraham of food writers, said that and meant it as a social, cultural statement.

'I can tell what class of person you are by what you eat.'

Savarin had fled from France because someone had said, 'let them eat cake', a statement that no one mistook as dietary advice.

The slim cartoon joke is far closer to what Savarin actually meant because you don't have to search very hard on your plate to realise that what we all eat is indeed other people. Their work, their expertise, their time, their aspirations, hopes and lives. We consume great steaming hot bowls full of people served up with a bewildering variety.

Restaurants are cutting-edge laboratories and theatres of cannibalism. At first glance you may look at a menu and imagine that what a restaurant serves is food, but you'd be wrong. What restaurants serve is people. People to people. You to the people on the table next door, the promise of you to the people booking a table for next week.

In every survey done on why people eat out, the food is never top of the list and hunger doesn't even get a mention. Don't be so naive as to imagine that all those people at the other tables are there because they are starving. We don't book a restaurant on the assumption of hunger, we book because we have a tribal herd need to suck the social marrow out of each other and consume the lives of people in far and distant countries whom we've never seen and rarely consider, except on a plate.

At this point I should insert a caveat, a disclaimer. This is not a scientific study, it's about behaviour, but I am not a behaviourist, I have no 'ism' to back up these assertions: this is committed prejudice based on a lot of observation, but it is not disinterested observation; I'm a professional, insatiable cannibal of human behaviour.

I have always thought that our pursuit of pleasure would be the most difficult thing to explain to an extra-terrestrial. Of all our pleasures, the most difficult would be our desire and joy in the taking of sustenance in company, with their elaborate rituals. After all, we don't seek the company of large groups of strangers to deposit waste or procreate or even get dressed. Of all intimate human behaviour, eating is the only one we seek company for. Indeed eating is, by its very nature, the oldest and strongest of our clannish origins.

Public eating is now, along with shopping, the most popular leisure activity in the West. Why? It is after all a very expensive and time-consuming way of seeing to rather simple bodily needs. The average meal in a London restaurant far exceeds the entire weekly budget for food and drink for an individual in this country. Part of the reason is of course ease.

The raw ingredients of dinner have over two generations become ever more plentiful and varied. Every year a new crop of strange-shaped and flavoured things arrives in supermarkets. The only people who can understand them, let alone peel them, are those who devote their professional time to cooking. The drift from home economics to specialist catering has made food a subject of mass obsession. It has always been a cause for snobbery and social distinction, but whereas class, manners and accents are removable and fixed, food is a continually shifting game.

It's all part of that lifestyle thing where once we had lives, now they come with a style and eating well is not eating what your grandfather ate, it's not even eating what you ate last week. The obsession with eating has elevated chefs and ingredients to the status of pop stars and songs, and they make about as much sense. Restaurants have become exclusive destinations, semi-private clubs.

Everything to do with food is a metaphor. To see the urban fetishism of restaurants, cookery books and celebrity chefs simply as a silly diversion is to see very little at all. It is to miss the point. Restaurants are the final cherry on the top of civilisation's cake. When you've got everything else right, then you can have a restaurant. The biblically begetting plethora of places to eat in Britain is a sign that socially, culturally, politically, economically, we've been getting quite a lot of that other stuff right. At heart restaurants are culture's rendezvous and its barometer.

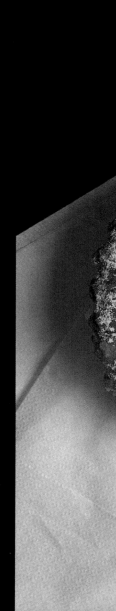

Starters

Starters

Salad

If anything has shot up the restaurant charts, it's salad. At Le Caprice, Caesar Salad is one of the top three starters. Even in the teeth of my prejudice against vegetables and salad, I must admit, it's a pretty perfect dish. A symbiotic mixture of ingredients. Le Caprice's is as good as it gets, unctuous without the extraneous additions like chicken breast or tuna. The habit of eating salad on its own as a separate course came from America, where else? There, the salad bar is still a weirdly staple-like feature of many restaurants. As many transatlantic media folk started asking for salads at lunch in Le Caprice, they invented a main course Mexican Chicken Salad, with avocado, the Arnold Schwarzenegger of green things. The plant that thinks it's a steak. If you were forced to live on just one ingredient (you can't), avocado would keep you miserably clinging to life longer than anything.

The attraction of salad is its perceived pristine freshness, its chlorophylliac, natural, animist goodness. Salad epitomises getting back to nature, it's the taste of Eden. Salad is our little plate of Arcadia, the herby banks of the Forest of Arden. A mixed leaf with olive oil and balsamico speaks to the Adam and Eve in each of you.

Which brings me to an odd conceit of restaurants. The al fresco fantasy. We associate food with outdoors. Naturally, food comes from outdoors, unless it comes from under the bed. Eating outdoors has a peculiar fascination, an attraction, for us. It's getting back to something, being reunited, reconnected. Even in a country as chronically unsuited to lunch without a roof as our own, the idea of the perfect picnic has a secret room all to itself in our heart. However foolish, however dangerous, we still have hunter-gatherer fantasies. You see office workers sitting on park benches in March, shivering over their lunch of a BLT bap, Twix and Styrofoam cappuccino.

Restaurants play on this fantasy. From Italian and Greek tavernas which daub landscapes on their walls to old-time posh restaurants which hang *faux* Dutch and Victorian landscapes on theirs. A restaurant that does have access to a real bit of outside, even if it's just the view of someone else's view will make the most of it. There is a piece of culinary algebra which says the better the view is, is in direct proportion to the nastiness of the food, and the expense of the bill. The more elaborate the table in the garden, with umbrellas, gas heaters, tablecloth clips etc., the longer and more likely the waiter is to forget all about you.

The one thing that most, no all, restaurants indulge your outdoor fantasies with is flowers. Often individual posies on the table and great elaborate floral confections on the bar or booking desk. Nobody ever comments on the flowers, no customer ever says 'we must go back there, they had lovely sweet williams', and in half a decade of reviewing, I don't think I have ever once mentioned the flowers in a restaurant, but they all have them and they spend as much as an extra waiter's salary on them. Why? I've nothing against flowers, but why do restaurants have to have them? Of course, restaurateurs will tell you it's all about colour and decoration.

A hundred years ago, Escoffier, one of the many fathers of cooking, said that everything on the table should be edible, or a direct aid to eating. He did away with all extraneous decorations, bits of silver, plaster-of-Paris castles, candles, generated cupids ringing bells, that sort of thing, and generally everybody saw the point and went along, except when it came to the flowers. Even in the very modernist of restaurants, where they've got rid of all the useful things as well, like carpets and curtains and good manners, there will still be flowers and when you think about it, that's very bizarre indeed. They are vegetables by birth, they are the lilies of the field that neither sow or reap, nor get boiled or turned into soup. We're going to chop and boil a few of your cousins and then chew them up and swallow them and we thought perhaps we'd put you in a vase here so that you can watch.

Flowers are a reminder of the wilderness that we and our food once came from and shared. They are also a trophy, a bouquet to nature controlled and tamed, like a captive. This, held in the prisons of our four walls, this stuff was dangerous, it was jungle and forest and wilderness, but see, here, now, it's just a rose in a vase.

The flowers on the table are a reminder of our lyrical past, but also of how far we've come. Safely cut off from their roots, it's okay. Heliotropes won't go for you, now we've got them indoors.

The flowers on your table, if you choose to notice, are the air you breathe and the food you eat. They are solid sunshine. The flowers at Le Caprice are, I'm afraid, something else. Here, they insist on exhibiting the most *outré* and somewhat trying installations. They won't be told. It's some sort of private boy thing, and perhaps I should just draw a veil and say no more, except baby food for the eye, if you get my drift.

Balsamic Dressing

A simple dressing for salads such as rocket or use with roasted or grilled vegetables.

200 ml extra-virgin olive oil

50 ml balsamic vinegar

salt and freshly ground black pepper

Whisk together the olive oil and balsamic vinegar and season.

Vinaigrette

For a classic French-style vinaigrette with a bit of body, whisk a couple of teaspoons of Dijon mustard into the strained Mimosa Dressing on page 72.

Chilli Dressing

A lightly spiced dressing that can be used for marinated meat or fish salads or simply to add a bit of heat to a simple vegetable salad.

150 ml extra-virgin olive oil

15 ml balsamic vinegar

25 ml sweet chilli sauce

1/4 tsp paprika

Whisk all of the ingredients together.

Mimosa Dressing

Use this dressing for green salads or delicate herb and lettuce leaves.

200 ml extra-virgin olive oil

2 cloves garlic, peeled

tarragon stalks (if using leaves in the salad) or tarragon sprigs

juice of 1 lemon

50 ml white wine vinegar

salt and white pepper

Make the dressing at least a day before you plan to use it.

Put the olive oil, garlic, tarragon, lemon juice and white wine vinegar into a bowl, season to taste and mix well.

Cover and leave at room temperature.

Leave the bits in to infuse further or strain them out.

Red Wine Dressing

Try to buy Cabernet Sauvignon vinegar; this is a rather special Spanish red wine vinegar, the best I have yet come across.

Alternatively use a good quality red wine vinegar. This dressing is ideal with robust salad leaves or with grilled meats and fish.

2 shallots, peeled and finely chopped

60 ml red wine vinegar

60 ml water

150 ml extra-virgin olive oil

salt and freshly ground black pepper

Simmer the shallots, red wine vinegar and water together until reduced by half.

Whisk in the olive oil and season with salt and pepper.

Roquefort Dressing

Particularly good with
salad leaves such as
endive or baby spinach.

Blend about 90 g of
Roquefort cheese with
the Vinaigrette recipe
on page 71.

Truffled Roseval Potatoes with Alsace Bacon

Roseval potatoes can be found during late summer. They have a pink skin and waxy flesh, which make them perfect for warm potato salads. As an alternative use Charlotte, Ratte or Pink Fir Apple. You may find Alsace bacon in a smart delicatessen (it has a luxurious smokey aroma and flavour), but otherwise use a good-quality smoked or cured streaky bacon, such as pancetta thinly sliced.

400–500 g Roseval potatoes

1 small black truffle, fresh or tinned, cleaned

30 ml balsamic vinegar

150 ml truffle oil

salt and freshly ground black pepper

250–300 g thinly sliced Alsace bacon, rind removed

Boil the Roseval potatoes in salted water for about 15 minutes until just cooked.

Drain them and leave to cool a little for about 5 minutes.

Meanwhile, finely chop the truffle and whisk it into the balsamic vinegar and truffle oil then season to taste.

Cut the potatoes in half and put into a bowl.

Mix them well, with half of the truffle dressing, then season with salt and pepper.

Leave to stand for about 1 hour to allow the truffle flavour to infuse the potato.

Pre-heat the grill and cook the slices of bacon until they are crisp. Arrange the potatoes on the plates, spoon on the rest of the dressing and top with the crispy bacon.

Belgian Endive Salad with Pommery Mustard Dressing

16 heads Belgian endive (chicory)

2 tbsps grain mustard

1 tbsp Dijon mustard

50 ml white wine vinegar

1/2 tbsp clear honey

150 ml extra-virgin olive oil mixed with 150 ml vegetable oil

salt and pepper

Cut the bottoms off the endives and remove any discoloured leaves.

Separate the leaves and wash them if necessary.

Whisk together the two mustards, the white wine vinegar and the honey.

Then gradually add the oils and season.

Toss the leaves in the dressing and serve the salad either in individual bowls or arranged on a plate.

1 x 1.5 kg duck or 12 duck legs

3 star anise

10 cloves garlic, roughly chopped

60 g fresh root ginger, roughly chopped

1 tsp five-spice powder

20 g coriander, stalks only, washed (use the leaves in the salad)

good vegetable oil for deep-frying

for the duck sauce

4 tbsps tomato ketchup

1 tsp honey

juice of 1/2 orange

1 tsp soy sauce

2 tbsps sesame oil

for the soy and sesame dressing

2 tsps soy sauce

2 tsps balsamic vinegar

1 clove garlic, peeled and crushed

10 g fresh root ginger, crushed

3 tbsps sesame oil

for the salad

4 bunches watercress, washed, picked over and stalks removed

110 g white radish (mooli), peeled and cut into 1 cm-wide ribbons

60 g bean shoots, washed

1 bunch spring onions, peeled, trimmed and quartered lengthways

20 g coriander leaves, from the duck recipe

2 tbsps sesame seeds, lightly toasted

60 g leek or fenugreek sprouts or similar (optional)

Crispy Duck and Watercress Salad

Cover the duck with water, add the herbs and spices, and bring to the boil. Simmer gently for 45 minutes.

Remove the duck from the stock and set it aside to cool. Skim the fat off the stock.

Whisk together all the ingredients for the duck sauce.

Put all the ingredients for the soy and sesame dressing into a blender and process until smooth.

To assemble the dish, remove the duck flesh from the bone, trim off any excess fat, but leave a little on.

Then cut into 1 cm-thick slices.

Pre-heat the oil to 160°C–180°C for deep-frying.

Arrange two-thirds of the watercress on the plates with the white radish, bean shoots and spring onions.

Deep-fry the duck until it is crisp, then drain it and mix with the duck sauce until it is nicely coated.

Arrange it in piles on the salad and spoon over the soy and sesame dressing.

Lastly, scatter the coriander and sesame seeds over the top and garnish with a small pile of the sprouts if available.

If you have already made the honey-baked Ham Hock (see page 106) this recipe is an ideal way of using the ham trimmings.

Alternatively, cook the ham and the lentils the day before you need them. Order dandelion in advance from your greengrocer or use curly endive as a second choice.

2 small ham hocks, each weighing 300–400 g, soaked in water overnight

1 small onion, peeled and roughly chopped

2 carrots, peeled, topped and tailed and left whole

10 peppercorns

4 cloves garlic, peeled

90 g Puy lentils, soaked for 2 hours in cold water

2 shallots, peeled and finely chopped

1 clove garlic, peeled and crushed

1 small carrot, peeled and finely diced

1 tbsp Dijon mustard

5 g parsley, washed and finely chopped

30 ml white wine vinegar

90 ml olive oil

salt and freshly ground black pepper

80–100 g dandelion leaves, washed and dried (or use an alternative such as rocket).

Ham Hock Salad
with Puy Lentils

Wash the ham hocks in cold water then put them into a large pot with the onion, carrots, peppercorns and garlic.

Cover with cold water, bring to the boil and simmer gently for 3–4 hours or until the meat comes away easily from the bone.

Remove from the heat and leave to cool.

If you're in a hurry, take the hocks out of the water and run them under the cold tap.

To make the dressing, cover the Puy lentils with plenty of cold water, bring to the boil, add a pinch of salt and simmer for 30–40 minutes.

To make sure they don't go mushy, test after 30 minutes.

(Cooking times vary with pulses, depending on how old and dry they are, so make sure they are done before you drain them.)

Put the shallots into a pan with the crushed garlic and carrots.

Add about 100 ml of the liquid the ham was cooked in and simmer for 5–6 minutes until the liquid has evaporated, then transfer them to a mixing bowl.

Stir in the mustard and parsley, then whisk in the white wine vinegar and olive oil.

Mix in the lentils and season with salt and pepper.

If the dressing looks a little thick, add a little more of the ham cooking liquid.

To serve the salad, remove the ham from the bone and flake it into small pieces, discarding any fat.

Put a couple of spoonfuls of dressing on each plate, scatter over some pieces of ham and a few dandelion leaves.

Fresh baby artichokes can be difficult to find so order them in advance from your greengrocer.

An alternative would be baby artichokes in olive oil, sometimes found in Italian food shops or supermarkets, but beware they are sometimes a little acidic.

16 baby artichokes

90 ml extra-virgin olive oil

3 cloves garlic, peeled and thinly sliced

10 g rosemary, leaves removed and chopped

juice of 1 lemon

60 ml white wine

salt and freshly ground black pepper

for the dressing

4 large shallots, peeled and finely chopped

120 ml Cabernet Sauvignon vinegar (or a good-quality red wine vinegar)

the olive oil from the artichoke cooking liquor (plus another 30–60 ml)

salt and freshly ground black pepper

to serve

150 g corn salad (also called lambs lettuce or salade mâche), carefully washed and dried

Poivrade **Artichoke** and **Mâche** Salad

Trim half the stalk from the artichokes and cut 1 cm off the top.

Peel the outer leaves off until you reach the pale-coloured green leaves in the centre, sometimes it may be only 6 leaves or so depending on the size of the artichokes.

Carefully slice each artichoke lengthways into 4 slices.

Put them into a saucepan (not aluminium as this will discolour the artichokes) and add the olive oil, garlic, rosemary, lemon juice and white wine.

Top up with water so that they are covered, season well with salt and pepper, bring to the boil then simmer for 7–8 minutes.

Remove from the heat and leave to cool.

The artichokes can be cooked the day before and left in the cooking liquor overnight.

Meanwhile make the dressing.

Simmer the shallots in the vinegar until reduced by two-thirds.

Once the artichokes are cooked, carefully remove the olive oil from the top with a ladle and whisk in to the shallots and vinegar.

Depending on how much oil you retrieve you may need to add a little extra.

Season with salt and pepper.

To serve, drain the artichokes from the cooking liquor and arrange on a plate with the corn salad. Spoon the dressing over the salad and artichokes.

Catalan Broad **Beans** with Chorizo **Sausage**

90 ml extra-virgin olive oil

2 small onions, peeled and finely chopped

4 cloves garlic, peeled and crushed

90 g small chorizo sausage, halved lengthways and sliced

2 tsps tomato purée

500 ml Chicken Stock (see page 35)

1 kg podded (2–2.5 kg unpodded) broad beans, fresh or frozen

15 g coriander, chopped

salt and freshly ground black pepper

Heat the olive oil in a saucepan and cook the onions and garlic until soft.

Stir in the chorizo, the tomato purée and the chicken stock.

Bring to the boil, season with salt and pepper and simmer for 30 minutes by which time the liquid will have reduced by about half.

Meanwhile, cook the broad beans for 5 minutes in boiling salted water (allow 2–3 minutes for frozen ones), drain then add them to the chorizo mixture and continue to simmer for a further 15 minutes.

If the liquid has evaporated add some more chicken stock or water.

Adjust the seasoning with salt and pepper, if necessary, stir through the coriander and serve.

Roasted **Italian Onions** with San Daniele Ham

A simple summer starter or light main course that Delia Smith included in her *Winter Collection*. Italian onions, or cipolline, are rather like squashed button onions, but if you can't find them use shallots.

80 ml extra-virgin olive oil

500 g flat Italian onions or shallots, peeled

salt and freshly ground black pepper

5 g thyme, leaves removed and chopped

50 ml balsamic vinegar

700–800 g thinly sliced San Daniele ham or prosciutto or parma

250–300 g young Provolone or Montasio cheese

Pre-heat the oven to 175°C/gas mark 4.

Heat a roasting tin in the oven for 10 minutes or so, then add 30 ml of the olive oil and the onions.

Season with salt and pepper and roast for 30–40 minutes.

After 20 minutes add the thyme and stir every so often until lightly coloured and soft. (Depending on the size of the onions or shallots the cooking time may vary.)

When the onions are ready add the balsamic vinegar to the pan, stir well and return it to the oven for 5 minutes so that the onions absorb some of the vinegar.

Remove from the oven and keep warm.

Drain any liquid from the onions into a bowl, mix it with the remaining olive oil and season to taste.

To serve, divide the onions between the plates and arrange the slices of ham on top.

With a potato-peeler take some thin shavings from the cheese and arrange them on the ham, then drizzle some of the dressing around.

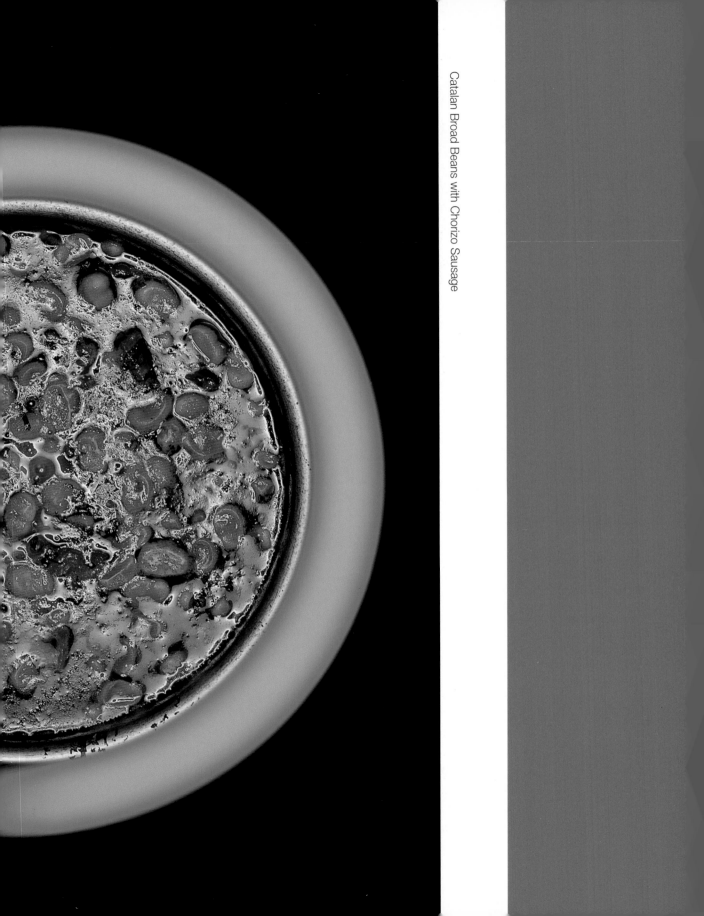

8 x 16-cm rounds puff pastry, rolled 3–4 mm thick

240 g sun-dried tomatoes in oil

2 tsps tomato purée

8 large, or 12 medium, ripe plum tomatoes, peeled and sliced

freshly ground black pepper

flaky rock salt

for the basil dressing

120 g basil leaves

150 ml extra-virgin olive oil

Plum **Tomato** and **Basil** Galette

Pre-heat the oven to 160°C/gas mark 3.

Prick the pastry bases with a fork and bake them for 7–8 minutes in the oven, turning them over after 2 minutes to ensure that the pastry does not rise. (If it does it will form an uneven base.)

Turn up the oven to 200°C/gas mark 6.

Drain most of the oil from the sun-dried tomatoes, then process them with the tomato purée in a blender until you have a fine paste.

Spoon it into a bowl.

Wash the blender, then make the dressing by processing the basil leaves with the olive oil.

Add a little more oil if the dressing looks too thick.

To assemble the galettes, spread a thin layer of the sun-dried tomato purée on the pastry bases.

Lay the sliced tomatoes in a circle on top, overlapping slightly.

Season with freshly ground black pepper and bake for 10–15 minutes.

Serve on warm plates.

Drizzle the basil dressing generously over the tomatoes and sprinkle with a pinch of rock salt.

Good-quality buffalo mozzarella is a must for this dish. When you compare the creaminess of buffalo with industrially produced mozzarella you'll know why!

Try to buy syrupy aged balsamic vinegar to finish the dish, as it makes all the difference.

1 clove garlic, peeled and crushed

5 g thyme, leaves removed and chopped

60 ml olive oil

salt and freshly ground black pepper

2 medium-sized aubergines, cut length-ways into 2-cm slices

1 kg buffalo mozzarella, left at room temperature

for the dressing

60 g capers, preferably in brine, rinsed in cold water

60 g stoned good-quality black olives, halved

90 g sun-dried tomatoes, cut into small dice

5 g fresh oregano or thyme, leaves removed

30 ml balsamic vinegar

90 ml extra-virgin olive oil

salt and freshly ground black pepper

to serve

50–60 ml aged balsamic vinegar

Buffalo **Mozzarella** with Baked **Aubergine** and Capers

Pre-heat the oven to 200°C/gas mark 6.

Mix together the garlic, thyme, olive oil and salt and pepper and spread it on to the slices of aubergine.

Heat a heavy frying-pan and cook them on both sides for a minute or so until golden, then put them on to a baking-tray and roast for 10 minutes until cooked through.

Meanwhile, make the dressing: mix together all the ingredients and season with salt and pepper.

Put the aubergines on to serving plates while they are still warm, spoon the dressing over and around them, then slice the mozzarella thickly and lay it on top.

Season with salt and pepper, then drizzle the aged balsamic vinegar around the plate.

Veal sweetbreads may be difficult to come by as their high cost means that butchers are reluctant to stock them.

Order them in advance and ask for the heart sweetbreads as they are plumper and easier to slice. As an alternative use lamb sweetbreads.

1 small onion, peeled and roughly chopped

1 carrot, peeled and roughly chopped

5 g thyme

1 bay leaf

10 black peppercorns

salt and freshly ground black pepper

1 kg veal sweetbreads

flour for dusting

30 ml vegetable oil

60 g butter

160–180 g baby spinach leaves

for the sauce gribiche

1 egg, hard-boiled and shelled

2 shallots, peeled and finely chopped

10 large gherkins, finely chopped

5 g parsley, washed and finely chopped

100 ml Vinaigrette (see page 71)

salt and freshly ground black pepper

Pan-fried Veal Sweetbreads with Sauce Gribiche

Put the onion, carrot, thyme, bay leaf and peppercorns into a saucepan with about a litre of water and 2 teaspoons of salt.

Bring to the boil and simmer for 30 minutes.

Add the sweetbreads to the pan, bring back to the boil and simmer for 6–7 minutes.

Take the pan off the heat and leave the sweetbreads to cool in the stock.

To make the sauce gribiche:

Push the hard-boiled egg through a coarse sieve or grate it. Mix carefully with the other ingredients and adjust the seasoning.

Remove the sweetbreads from the cooking liquor, peel away the outer membrane then cut them into 1-cm thick slices.

Dry them with kitchen paper, then season with salt and pepper and flour them lightly.

Heat the vegetable oil in a heavy frying-pan, add the butter and when it

starts to foam put in the sweetbreads and cook for 2–3 minutes on each side until they are crisp.

Arrange the baby spinach leaves on a plate, spoon the sauce around then top with the sweetbreads.

A great summer risotto. If you grow your own courgettes and don't know what to do with all the flowers that appear with no courgettes on them, here's the answer.

60 ml olive oil

4 shallots, peeled and finely chopped

5 g thyme, leaves removed and chopped

400 g carnaroli rice

1 ltr hot Vegetable Stock (see page 35)

6 medium courgettes, cut into 1-cm dice

16 courgette flowers, if available

5 g parsley, finely chopped

60 ml double cream

60 g butter

60 g Pecorino Romano, grated

Risotto with Zucchini and Pecorino

Heat the olive oil in a thick-bottomed pan and cook the shallots and thyme in it for a few minutes until they are soft, but not coloured.

Add the rice and stir it well with a wooden spoon.

Gradually add the hot stock, a little at a time, stirring constantly and ensuring that each addition has been fully absorbed by the rice before adding the next.

Meanwhile, cook the diced courgettes in a little of the vegetable stock for 1 minute, then drain.

When the rice is almost done, add the courgettes and the flowers, and keep adding stock until the rice is soft and plump: the risotto should be quite moist.

Then stir in the chopped parsley, the cream and the butter.

Taste and adjust the seasoning.

You can serve the risotto with the Pecorino sprinkled on top, or with it stirred in.

Do not try to use preserved truffles for this recipe as there will be no comparison in flavour.

It would be like serving Babycham instead of Champagne.

for the mushroom stock

2 onions, peeled and roughly chopped

1 leek, trimmed, washed and roughly chopped

1 clove garlic, peeled and roughly chopped

30 ml vegetable oil

500 g button mushrooms, washed and roughly chopped

30 g dried ceps, soaked for 1 hour in a little warm water

10 g thyme

10 black peppercorns

1 bay leaf

for the risotto

60 g butter

400 g carnaroli rice

1–1.5 ltrs hot mushroom stock

salt and freshly ground white pepper

120 ml champagne

60 g butter

60 ml double cream

80–100 g fresh black truffles

Champagne **Risotto** with Perigord **Truffles**

First make the stock. Gently cook the onions, leek and garlic in the vegetable oil without colouring until soft.

Add the rest of the ingredients, then pour in about 2 litres of water, bring to the boil and simmer for 1 hour, skimming occasionally.

Strain through a fine-meshed sieve and keep hot if using straight away.

The stock should be strong in flavour: if it is not, reduce it until the flavour is concentrated.

You should be left with about 1.5 litres.

To make the risotto, take a thick-bottomed pan, melt the butter in it and add the rice.

Stir for a minute on a low heat with a wooden spoon.

Gradually add the stock a little at a time, stirring constantly and ensuring that each addition has been fully absorbed by the rice before adding the next.

Season with salt and pepper.

The risotto should be of a moist consistency, not too stodgy.

When the rice is almost cooked, add the champagne and continue to stir for a few minutes.

Add the butter and cream, check the seasoning again and correct if necessary.

Meanwhile wash the truffles briefly and brush away any soil with a small brush.

Spoon the risotto on to the plates and shave the truffles directly on top, using a special truffle-shaver, mandolin, or a good vegetable peeler.

If langoustines are not available, use cooked lobster and allow 90 g of shelled meat per person.

60–70 medium-sized langoustines, live if possible

vegetable oil for frying

6 medium shallots, peeled and roughly chopped

4 cloves garlic, peeled and roughly chopped

30 g butter

5 g thyme, leaves and stalks roughly chopped

1 bay leaf

2 tsps plain flour

2 tsps tomato purée

a pinch of saffron strands

60 ml white wine

200 ml Fish Stock (see page 35)

200 ml double cream

600 g good-quality dried fettuccini

5 g tarragon, leaves removed and chopped

salt and freshly ground black pepper

Fettuccini
with Langoustine Tails

Bring a large pan of salted water to the boil.

Plunge in the langoustines, and bring the water back to the boil and simmer for 2 minutes.

Drain the langoustines in a colander and leave them to cool a little: you will find them easier to peel while they are still warm.

Remove the heads, then remove the meat from the tails by gently squeezing the shell together until it cracks, then prising it open.

Put the meat to one side in a bowl.

To make the sauce, break up the shells a little with a meat bat or the bottom of a saucepan.

Heat the vegetable oil in a thick-bottomed pan then fry the shells with the shallots and garlic for 5–10 minutes until lightly coloured.

Add the butter, thyme and bay leaf, then stir in the flour and tomato purée.

Add the saffron, then slowly stir in the white wine and fish stock, bring to the boil and simmer for 45 minutes.

The sauce should have reduced by half.

Add the double cream then continue to simmer for 10 minutes or so until the sauce thickens again.

Strain through a colander, pushing the sauce through with a spoon.

Process it in a blender until it is smooth.

Cook the pasta in boiling salted water until it is *al dente* then drain.

Reheat the peeled langoustine tails in the sauce with the tarragon, taste and adjust the seasoning, then toss with the pasta and serve immediately.

It's not really worth going to the trouble of making fresh pasta for this dish so buy good-quality dried cannelloni or lasagne sheets and roll them yourselves.

for the pea purée

30 g butter

1 small onion, peeled and finely chopped

1 kg frozen peas

150 ml Vegetable Stock (see page 35)

10 g mint leaves

salt and freshly ground black pepper

for the cannelloni

1 ltr double cream

90 g freshly grated Parmesan

salt and freshly ground black pepper

1 egg yolk

16 pieces good-quality cannelloni or 16 lasagne sheets

120–150 g gorgonzola, cut into small cubes

Cannelloni with Peas and Gorgonzola

Pre-heat the oven to 230°C/gas mark 8.

First make the pea purée.

Heat the butter in a saucepan and cook the onion gently until soft.

Add the peas, vegetable stock and mint, season, and simmer for 10–12 minutes.

Purée in a blender until smooth.

Check and correct the seasoning.

Line a colander with a clean tea-towel or a piece of muslin, pour in the pea purée and leave to drain for an hour or so to get rid of any excess water.

Meanwhile, bring the double cream to the boil and simmer until it has reduced in volume by half.

Add the Parmesan cheese and stir until it has dissolved.

Season with salt and pepper, allow to cool a little then whisk in the egg yolk.

Cook the cannelloni (manufacturers' cooking times will vary), refresh it in a little cold water and drain.

Fill the cannelloni with the pea purée (a piping bag will help), and arrange in an ovenproof dish.

Stir the gorgonzola into the sauce and pour it over the cannelloni.

Bake for 10–15 minutes, or until golden.

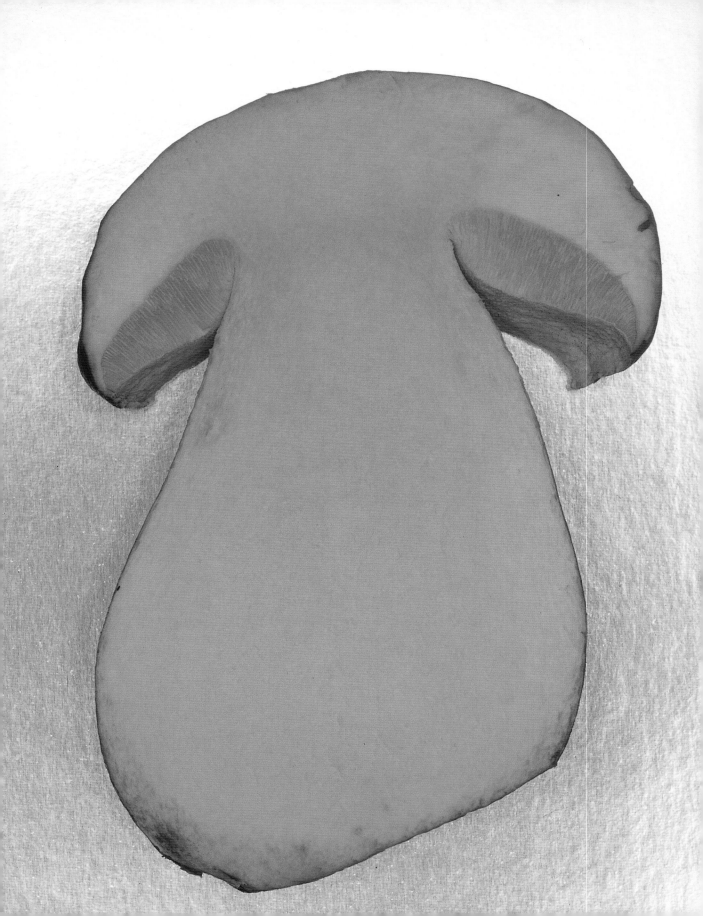

Tagliatelle
with
Ceps

Use fresh ceps, not dried, as the end result will be disappointing.

Alternatively, use another type of wild mushroom.

800 g fresh ceps

30 ml olive oil

2 cloves garlic, peeled and crushed

400 ml mushroom stock

200 ml double cream

400 g good-quality dried tagliatelle

10 g parsley, washed and finely chopped

90 g unsalted butter

salt and freshly ground black pepper

If the ceps are very dirty, wash them briefly in a bowl of water and scrape off the sand or earth with a small knife. Dry them on kitchen paper, then cut them into $\frac{1}{2}$-cm slices.

Heat the olive oil in a frying-pan until almost smoking, then sauté the ceps a handful at a time with the crushed garlic until lightly coloured.

Drain them in a colander, reserving any liquid for the sauce.

Reduce the mushroom stock with any liquid from the ceps until it has almost evaporated.

Add the cream and reduce again by about half until the sauce thickens.

Meanwhile cook the pasta in boiling salted water until it is *al dente*, then drain.

Add the ceps, parsley and butter to the sauce and bring it back to the boil.

Toss the sauce with the pasta and adjust the seasoning with salt and pepper.

Atmosphere

There is this noise, a particular undulating ambient hum, like a human steam train. I'd recognise it anywhere, in any language, in any room in the world. It is the most attractive, whinnying, more-ish sound. It's the sound of a contented, convivial restaurant, working, well-oiled, tuned, confident. Nobody's too drunk, nor too sober, there aren't too many tables of single testosterone-rich bankers or career women out on a single girls' moan. The waiters are stoking in time to the rhythm of consumption, there are enough couples who fancy each other and want to talk about it and enough matched tables who are truly pleased to see each other. The laughter isn't strident and the sound level never rises to a shout and never falls so that you can hear the conversation next to you. It is the most complicated recipe, you can't measure the ingredients or write it down. You can't teach it and what works in one room will be poison in another, but if you can manage it, properly manage it, conjure it up, it's money in the bank, and a queue in the reservations book. It is the closest thing you'll ever hear outside of a playground to the sound of joy.

Forget 'location, location, location'. You can bet your service charge that whoever said that didn't eat in his own restaurants. The three most important rules for a successful restaurant are 'atmosphere, atmosphere, atmosphere'. Le Caprice's location is up a cul-de-sac, with no passing trade, and it could be as dead as any cul-de-sac in London, but the taxis beat a path to do U-turns at its door because seven nights a week it can produce that noise out of a list of intangibles and thin air.

Ask most people what makes them choose one restaurant over another and the answer is atmosphere. If they work in the PR business, they'll probably call it ambience. Atmosphere always comes above food as a reason for choosing a restaurant, but of course it's the one thing you can't send back. You can't ask the waiter to turn up the atmosphere or demand a refund on the underdone ambience. Although everyone knows what a good atmosphere is what you bring with you. It's a mutually symbiotic exchange between customers. Really the restaurant's only charging you corkage with the food. It's a match of mood and expectation. Sitting beside people who are having a raucous good time is as depressing as sitting opposite a couple who have only exchanged half a dozen words in the last month. The silent dining couple is the bane of all restaurant managers, sat in the middle of the room avoiding eye contact, staring into the middle distance, chewing in solitary unison like over-milked Friesians – they can suck up atmosphere and turn it into distilled mud.

The abiding love and veneration the English had with the indigenous French and Italian restaurants wasn't, when all's said and done, about their food which was generally no better than fine, it was the floor show, the effortless sense of occasion southern Europeans brought to even drinking a cup of coffee. We loved it, just sitting and soaking up the atmosphere and griping, 'why can't there be places like this back home? I'm up for it.'

Well, we weren't. Just the fact that we sat and watched showed we weren't. We all thought that continental entertainment was a spectator sport, we paid to be entertained, but we never thought where the rest of the cast came from.

We're getting better. Certainly in big cities we are less easily intimidated and more relaxed, more knowledgeable, less defensive. Restaurants have done as much to mould and liberate and soften our national character as anything else since the war.

> If someone had come to me five years ago and said:
> **'Hit or miss?**
> Sushi made by robot and served on a conveyor belt?
> Tunisian food, served on infant-school tables and chairs,
> with deafening North-African Euro rock?
> Japanese-Peruvian food?'
> And I'd have said, without having to think much,
> **'Miss, miss and miss.'**
> And I'd have been wrong, wrong and wrong.

They all caught on, they all got the atmosphere. What makes eating out successful, what makes restaurants, what gives restaurants that hum is as intangible as what makes a good novel or a successful film or a moving symphony. Restaurants are culture, not just catering.

Part of the joy of eating in restaurants is the unpredictability, the weird, unlikely combination of ingredients that go into the recipe that make up a successful restaurant. They are like your address book. You look at all those names and there is no common denominator, except that you love them but you can't remember or imagine why.

Altogether, restaurants are the outward reflection of who you are and the things that make a good restaurant somehow manage to be for a night, for a couple of hours, a reflection and a distillation of the person you would like to be, as it will be for a hundred other disparate customers. For one dinner, you will belong to the same family, the same clan, the same club. The noise and that buzz is so attractive, is so more-ish, because in a world where so much alienates, this makes you feel like you belong.

Main Courses

well, it's something of a wonder that we are still eating meat at all. Nothing, with the possible exception of class-A drugs and boxing has received such sustained bad publicity as meat. Mad, bad and dangerous to chew. Everything that could go wrong for muscle and sinew has for meat: poisonous cancers, insane, cruel, manipulated, injected, tortured, gross, sad, smelly, colon-clogging, bleeding meat.

Factory-produced meat is a mass of contradictions. It's seen as being worthlessly cheap while at the same time costing a lot. It's perceived as man-manufactured when it is actually as natural as you are. Meat is so despised that it is the only material I can think of where the man-made nylon-textured protein material is considered preferable to the real thing.

Altogether the faddism of meat, whether true, half-true or plain bogus, isn't the point but is an excuse. You're spoiling for a fight with meat. We want our prejudices reconfirmed. The facts don't really matter as much as the perception and the truth, the big gut truth, is that meat doesn't fit in with who we want to be. It represents everything we want to distance ourselves from. It's old fashioned, it's paternalistic, it's final and corrupt, it's autocratic men standing at the head of tables with knives dripping blood, it's wasteful and polluting and cruel and as our feelings about nature become ever more anthropomorphic and sentimental so meat gets to be closer and closer to being murder and whole earth cannibalism. If anything was the physical symbol of the attitude we want to leave behind it is dead cooked cows on a trolley. But this leaves us with a problem, we are all carnivorous. We are just born that way. Smile at the mirror and your mouth betrays your true, dark nature. Those eye teeth, the ripping, puncturing, carnivorous teeth. Kiss your lover with all the tender, pluralistic, non-judgmental, equitable, un-sexist sexuality and passive engagement you can muster and there in the salivary dark is sharp proof of your bloody nature. Kissing by the way is interesting. Open-mouth passionate kissing is exciting and dangerous because it mimics ravenous consuming. You put your tongue, that delicate, complex, soft, vulnerable and irreplaceable bit of communicating, tasting kit into another mouth this close to the hard slicing ivory. Every kiss is an act of trust, an offering to the vulnerability that mimics eating. There is a hint of a praying mantis courtship in every sexual encounter. We talk of being consumed by love, of hungering for loved ones. Sex is a carnivorous appetite.

Meat carries more of the burden of metaphor food than any other ingredient. It's death and corruption there in front of you, a reminder of your own inescapable demise. In fairness, the squeamishness about meat is not new. It's not entirely a pseudo-scientific medical product of the post-war, post-hunger, self-obsessed generation. It has always been treated with a wary respect. Meat was what you gave up to become closer to God. Lenten fasts, Fridays, indeed the old Catholic fast days amounted to a third of the year. No meat to remind your own roasting in the fires down below. Rabbits, by the way, were honorary fish for the purpose of fasting and bizarrely, puffins were honorary rabbits because they lived in holes in the ground but at a time when societies that dined had a complex and vociferous spiritual life, when we believed in something rather than just everything. There was the balancing belief in resurrection, meat died so that you could live in your bone and muscle and vigour. We gave up meat for Lent but slaughter the Paschal lamb for Easter.

Now we don't believe in the divine mystery and contrarily have given animals souls, that presumably aren't going anywhere. The death of our dinner was always a symbol for our mortality. In fact the blood and the squealing were central to the hard inescapable fact of life because the avoidance of death has become part and parcel of the modern obsession with the medicinal quality of food and the cholesterol within meat is a symbol too far, it is too uncomfortable.

We don't have the spiritual, moral, psychological faith to deal with meat on a plate, so we'd rather not think about it. Death is no longer a natural comma in a temporal, spiritual life. It's a full stop and a mistake and a fault. We believe against belief that life should and perhaps could run on like a sentence without punctuation for ever. Experience and logic may tell us that we will get to the end of the page but the actual divided cell, or unseen bug, or worn-out valve that carries us over is a fault that could have been corrected, foreseen or circumnavigated. The absence of life is inevitable but the means of death is avoidable. This tautology, this absurd piece of modern fearful hopeless logic is borne on the backs of our daily meat. Don't eat death and you won't catch death, which is something of a problem for restaurants.

I've chosen to trace the origin of the restaurant proper from the French Revolution and the new ideas of *égalité* and *fraternité* coupled with the beginning of modern husbandry and the industrial revolution. Democracy, free speech and technology come together to make public leisured eating possible but there is an older heritage; through inns, fairs and the difficult necessities of travelling, there have always been places to eat in public because there has always been a need to eat on the road or in places where you don't have relatives. These aren't restaurants as we understand them because in a restaurant the food is central but incidental. A restaurant is a bourgeois advertisement. It's a choice amongst choices, not a necessity. The older public eating was usually without choice. You ate what was being cooked.

Fairs and markets and ports were where you found public eating and one of its most important facets was cooking meat. The only time a lot of people would eat from large joints of meat was at public fairs and markets. The rotating of whole animals was something that you need a crowd for in rural communities. Meat was eked out, preserved or sold, so meat-eating became special and festive in mediaeval Europe. It became the monopoly of guilds. There was a court case in Paris where an inn wanted to offer a menu to drinkers, actually a dish of calves' tongues in white sauce, and was taken to court by the guild of public victual purveyors as an infringement of practice. The inn won and technically became the first ever restaurant. It was strangely called The London Bridge.

Large joints of meat were so expensive and such a profligate use of meagre resources that eating it was almost always a communal extravagance except for the richest households. The Tudor and Stuart court ate meat almost to the exclusion of all other ingredients as a symbol of kingship, nobility and power, giving Henry VIII gout. As a result, the public festive sense of eating large bits of meat in public has survived to the present day in the carvery's chariot that is ritually wheeled through restaurants, with its ribs of beef or baron of lamb, by an imposing chef in a high toque. The etiquette of tipping the server is perhaps left over from the mediaeval practice of offering a bribe for the best cuts. The derided modern hotel carvery is in a direct line from the ancient market or saint's festival banquet. All courses on show at once, a visual display of imposing excess and communal gluttony. But the carvery and chariot are already old-fashioned, making way for the antipasto and salad bar and kitchen-plated dinner.

Restaurants have a problem with meat. Look at menus over the last ten years and you see meat dishes decline. Twenty years ago every restaurant had to offer steak, plain or garnished, with minimal vegetables. Perhaps there would be two or three cuts of steak. It was there because there was a sizeable proportion of the population who only ate steak. Eating out was eating steak, a special occasion. A restaurant meal had to be a slab of meat.

Despite the publicity and the fear and fashion, meat persists because it just tastes so damn good. We are built to eat meat. The combination of fat and muscle and blood is delicious in a way that nothing else can mimic. Vegetarianism is not a garden path many of us can be led up for long, so we want to eat meat but we don't want to catch ourselves eating meat and cooks want to cook meat, they want to cook meat very, very badly. Cookery without meat is Macbeth without murder. Meat is the central discipline of cookery, everything else is accompaniment or a support band. Nothing is as robust, as versatile, as talented as meat. The truth about chefs is that they don't care what you eat, they don't really care if you like what you eat, they care about their craft. They'd still cook meat if nobody ordered it, they'd cook meat in secret if it was illegal, in fact when meat on the bone and bits of cow offal were illegal, chefs all over London still cooked it for themselves for pleasure and pride. You look at most expensive menus and you'll see a dish that you know hardly anyone ever orders – tripe or calves' head or thymus glands in white sauce. It's there because it's what the chef does. It's a plate of his self-worth.

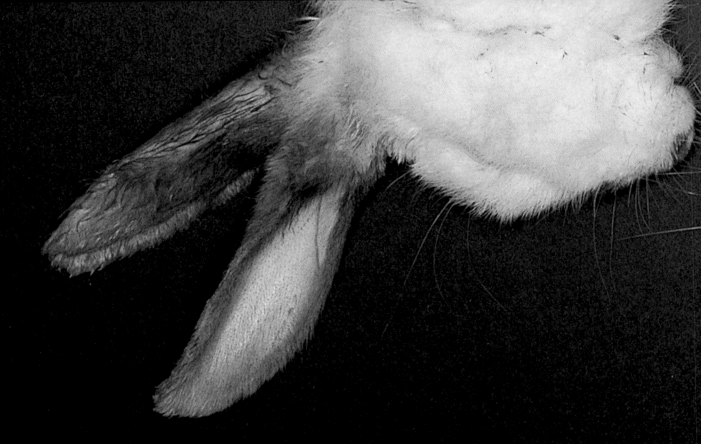

The rule with meat used to be that the better the pasture the simpler the cooking. In the wet north of Europe we have excellent grass and wonderful beef and lamb and plentiful game so cooking was big bits of meat roasted or boiled simply. In the south, grazing was limited and feed expensive so meat was used more sparingly and prepared with greater invention through necessity. But the growing popularity of southern European cookery and the health and dietary scares have meant that meat on menus comes in smaller bits, shyly hidden in amongst the vegetables and sauces. This has changed the way butchers prepare meat. Continental butchery, sometimes called 'seam butchery', is based on muscle groups, so individual muscles are filleted along their seams like unpicking a suit. Cuts tend to be small and have fat from other animals added to them. This suits restaurants because they cook quicker and there is a perceived added value in the preparation. English butchery is skeletal, that is carcasses are jointed and the thinnest part of the bone cut so the muscle is cooked on the bone which is good for eating but means that the cuts are much bigger. Traditional English butchery is dying out. Few of us are ordering a 'Northumberland duck '(made from lamb), an 'oven buster' or a 'Jacob's ladder'. Today we want meat that tastes vaguely meaty but doesn't appear mammalish. It's not only because meat is bad for you – lots of things you do are bad for you – it's that meat says bad things about you. Every plate of meat has to be accompanied by the social workers of vegetable and served in amenable, non-threatening pieces. Meat is just too overtly, unreconstructedly blokeish when proto-humanity was divided between the hunters and the gatherers.

'Rabbits, by the way, were honorary fish for the purpose of fasting.'

Try to buy fresh baby beetroot for this dish: you may need to pre-order them from your greengrocer. Otherwise use normal beetroot and cut it into quarters. Cook the meats and prepare the beetroot the day before so that they have time to chill and are ready to serve.

1 salted ox tongue, about 800 g–1 kg (or buy ready-cooked tongue)

1 onion, peeled and halved

2 carrots, peeled and trimmed

10 black peppercorns

1 bay leaf

vegetable oil for roasting

500–600 g veal topside or loin

1 kg baby beetroot

salt and freshly ground black pepper

250 ml balsamic vinegar

5 g thyme, leaves removed and chopped

30 g caster sugar

60 ml extra-virgin olive oil

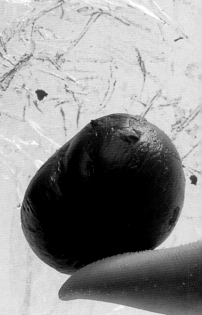

Put the ox tongue into a large saucepan with the onion, carrots, peppercorns and bay leaf.

Bring to the boil and simmer for about 2–2 1/2 hours.

Leave to cool in the liquid, but while it is still warm, peel away the skin with your fingers, then return the tongue to the cooking liquid.

Pre-heat the oven to 220°C/gas mark 7.

Heat a little vegetable oil in a roasting tray in the oven for about 10 mins.

Season the veal and cook it in the roasting tray for about 1 hour, turning and basting it 3 or 4 times during cooking.

Test it by inserting a skewer or carving fork into the centre of the meat for 10 seconds: when it is done, the tip of the skewer or tines should be warm.

The veal should be cooked medium rare so that it remains moist.

Put it to one side to cool.

Cook the beetroot in their skins in salted water for 50–60 minutes, depending on their size, then test them with the point of a sharp knife.

Once cooked, allow them to cool then rub the skins with your hands, wearing a pair of rubber gloves.

If using large beetroot cut them into 4.

Bring the balsamic vinegar to the boil with the thyme and sugar.

Allow it to cool, then pour it over the beetroot and leave.

To serve, cut the meats thinly with a sharp knife and arrange on the plates.

You can serve the beetroot separately or on the plates.

Drizzle with olive oil and grind over some black pepper.

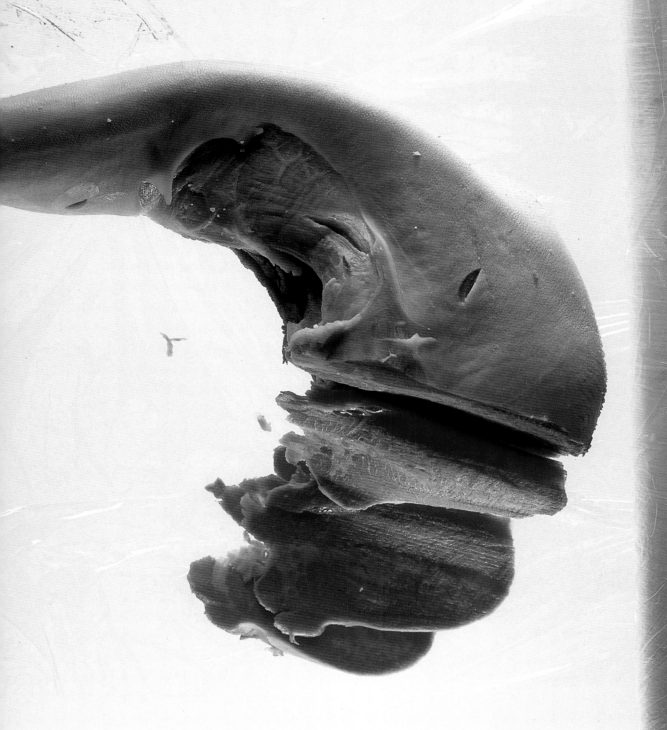

Cold **Ox Tongue** and **Veal** with Baby Beetroots and Balsamico

The way this dish is served in the restaurant is quite wasteful as only the centre of the ham hock is used, the rest is then used for a ham hock salad. So if you have a large enough pot to make this dish, save the trimmings and freeze them. Or simply serve half a hock per person although it won't look as good.

8 unsmoked ham hocks or knuckles, weighing 300–400 g each, soaked overnight in water to remove any excess salt

3 onions, peeled and roughly chopped

3 carrots, peeled and roughly chopped

1 bay leaf

5 cloves

1 tsp black peppercorns

5 g thyme

for the sauce

3-4 large shallots, peeled and finely chopped

1 tbsp English mustard

90 ml white wine

300 ml Chicken Stock (see page 35), reduced by two-thirds

90 ml double cream

2 tsps grain mustard

salt and freshly ground black pepper

for the glaze

300 g clear honey

100 g grain mustard

to serve

Mashed Potato

Honey Baked **Ham Hock** with Mustard Sauce

Wash the ham hocks in cold water and put them into a large pot with the onions, carrots, bay leaf, cloves, peppercorns and thyme.

Cover with cold water, bring to the boil and simmer for 3 hours.

Remove the hocks from the cooking liquid and leave to cool.

To make the sauce:

Simmer the shallots, English mustard and white wine together until completely reduced.

Add the chicken stock and continue to simmer until the sauce has reduced by half, add the double cream and grain mustard and simmer until the sauce thickens. Season to taste.

Once the ham hocks are cool enough to handle (you can cheat and run them under cold water) remove and discard the fat, then carefully remove the outer section of meat and the large bone, leaving the small bone attached to the centre eye of meat.

Preheat the oven to 200°C/gas mark 6.

For the glaze, mix together the honey and mustard to form a paste.

Put the ham hocks into a baking tray lined with tin foil to prevent the tray burning, then spread the honey over them.

Bake for about 30 minutes, basting the hocks every so often until they are golden.

Bring the sauce back to the boil. Heat the mashed potato.

Serve the hock on the mashed potato with the sauce poured around.

80 g butter

8 medium-sized onions,
peeled and
thinly sliced

5 g thyme, leaves
removed and chopped

60 g flour

60 ml dry cider

1.5 ltrs Chicken Stock
(see page 35)

1.5 kg tripe,
washed and cut into
6–8 cm pieces

salt and freshly ground
white pepper

60 ml double cream

Tripe and Onions

Melt the butter in a thick-bottomed pan and sweat the onions and thyme with the lid on until soft.

If the onions begin to colour add a tablespoon of water to the pan and stir well.

Then add the flour, stir it in and cook on a low heat for another minute.

Gradually pour in the cider and chicken stock, stirring constantly.

Bring to the boil, add the tripe, season with salt and pepper and simmer gently for 1 hour until tender.

If the sauce seems to be getting too thick, add a little more stock or water.

Different types of tripe will have different cooking times so keep an eye on it.

When the recipe is done, stir in the double cream and check the seasoning.

Serve with a good helping of mashed potato.

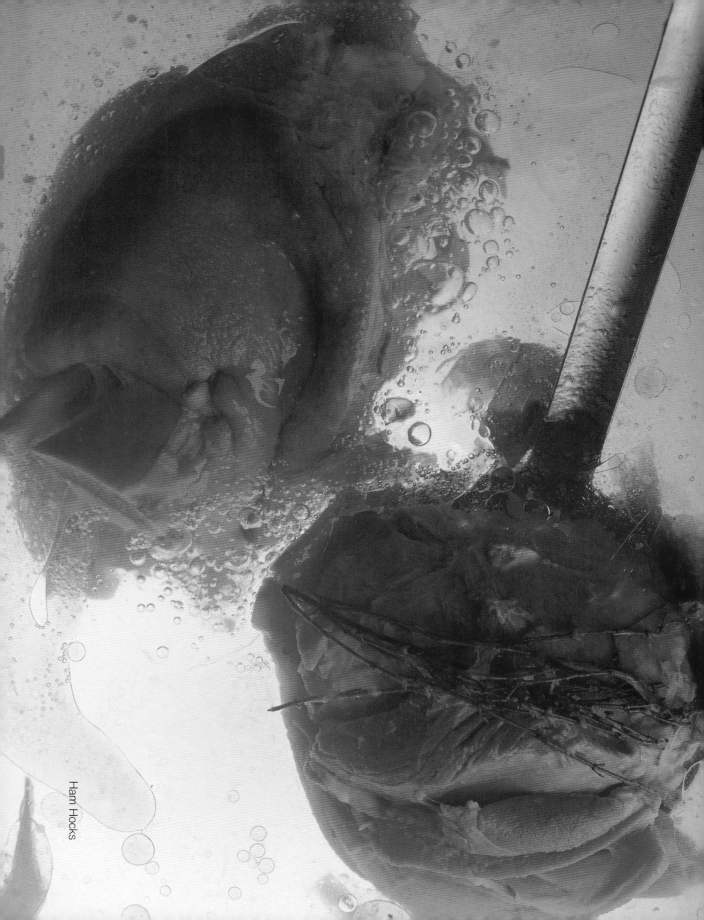

Ham Hocks

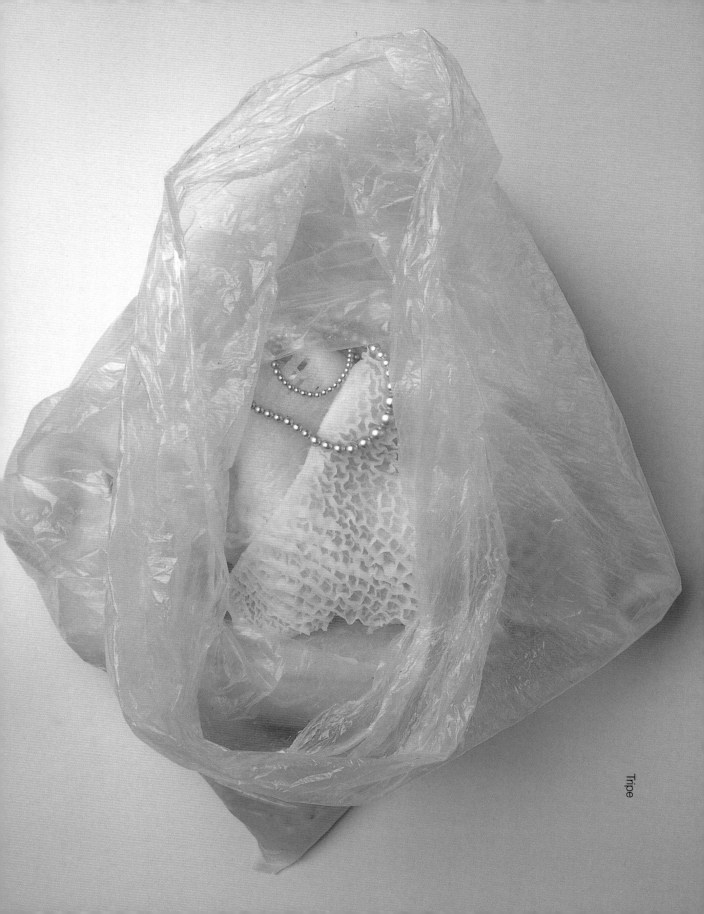

Game birds are best cooked and served simply, be they partridge, grouse or pheasant. A quick, hot cooking will keep smaller birds pink and moist.

Hanging is up to individual tastes, but stronger game, like grouse, will naturally have a distinctive flavour and need not be hung for too long.

Partridge, either grey or red-legged, will improve with longer hanging.

We have given a simple classic recipe for roast partridge and bread sauce, which will do for most birds.

Browned breadcrumbs and liver croûtes may add a classic touch to grouse and woodcock (but that's up to you!)

vegetable oil for deep frying

3 large clean parsnips

200 ml Dark Meat Stock (see page 34)

200 ml Chicken Stock (see page 35)

8 partridge

salt and pepper

butter

100 ml red wine

cornflour (optional)

Roasting **Game** Birds

Pre-heat the oven to 240°C/gas mark 9.

Heat some oil to 180°C in a deep-fat fryer.

Top and tail the parsnips, leaving the skin on unless it's very brown, then slice them as thinly as possible lengthways (with a mandolin, if you have one), then dry them with a clean tea-towel.

Fry the slices in the hot oil a few at a time, stirring to ensure that they don't stick together.

They will take a while to colour and may appear soft while they are still in the fat but once they have been drained they will dry out and crisp up.

Leave them somewhere warm, but not hot, to dry.

Reduce the two stocks together by two-thirds.

Lightly season the partridges and rub the breasts with a little softened butter.

Roast them in the oven for about 15 minutes.

If you insert a sharp knife or carving fork between the legs and breast a little blood should run out.

Slightly pink is the ideal way to serve partridge or they will be a bit dry.

Put the partridges on a plate to rest and to catch any juices that run out. Place the roasting tin in which they were cooked over a low heat, add the red wine and stir the bottom to remove any cooking residue.

Reduce the red wine until almost completely evaporated and pour in the stock.

Simmer for a few minutes, then strain the gravy through a fine-meshed sieve into a small pan and season to taste.

It should be thick enough now but, if not, mix a little cornflour with water and stir it in.

The partridges can be served whole or with the breasts and legs cut off the carcasses.

Hand the bread sauce, parsnip chips and gravy separately.

Brussels sprouts with chestnuts would make an excellent accompaniment.

Liver Croûtes

Game birds are rarely sold with the livers in these days. If you buy your game from a specialist butcher or game dealer then ask for the livers to be kept.

livers from the bird, cleaned

120 g chicken livers, cleaned

salt and freshly ground black pepper

1 tbsp cognac

60 g butter

8 x 1/2-cm slices of white baguette

Season both of the livers with salt and pepper.

Heat the butter in a frying-pan until foaming, add the livers and cook for a minute on each side on a high heat.

Add the cognac to the pan and remove from the heat, don't be alarmed if the livers ignite, this is just the alcohol burning off the cognac.

Blend the livers briefly in a food-processor, the mixture should be a little coarse, and transfer to a bowl. Leave to cool.

To serve, toast the slices of baguette on both sides, warm the liver mixture and spread on generously, about 1/2–1 cm thick.

Serve the liver croûtes on the plate with the bird.

Bread Sauce

1 medium onion, peeled and halved

100 g butter

6 cloves

1 bay leaf

1 ltr milk

1/2 tsp ground nutmeg

salt and freshly ground white pepper

200 g fresh white breadcrumbs

Finely chop half of the onion and cook gently in 50 g of the butter until soft.

Stud the other half with the cloves, pushing them through the bay leaf to anchor it.

Put the milk, nutmeg and studded onion into the pan with the cooked onion and bring it to the boil.

Season then simmer for 30 minutes.

Remove the pan from the heat and leave the milk to infuse for 30 minutes or so.

Take out and discard the studded onion.

Add the breadcrumbs and return the sauce to a low heat.

Simmer for 15 minutes, giving it the occasional stir.

Pour a third of the bread sauce from the pan into the blender and liquidise, then return it to the pan

and add the remaining 50 g butter.

Stir until the sauce has amalgamated, then check and correct the seasoning.

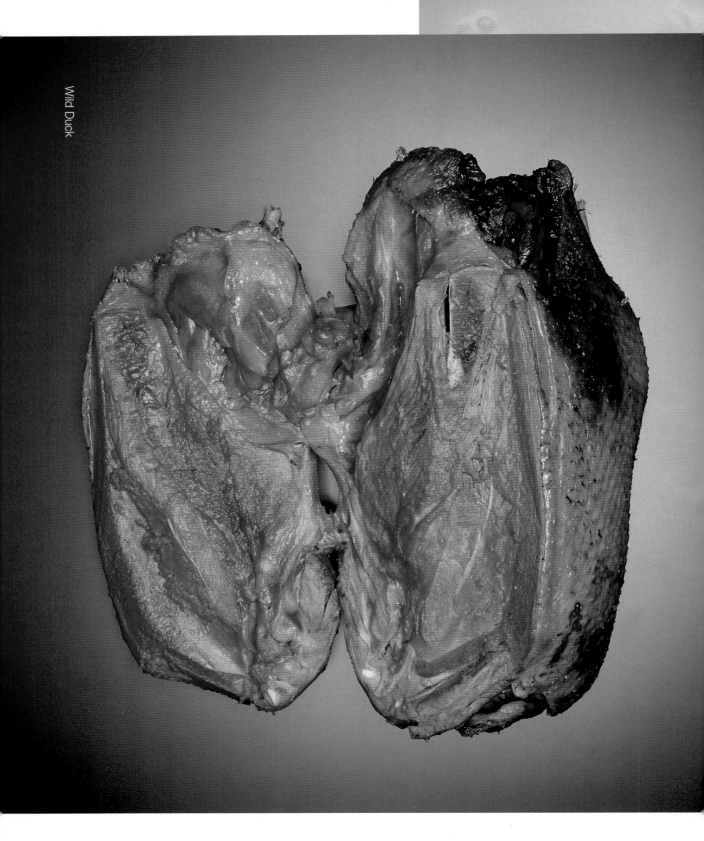

2 medium red onions, peeled and finely chopped

250 ml red wine

500 ml Dark Meat Stock (see page 34), reduced by two-thirds

2 medium-sized cauliflowers, cooked whole in boiling salted water

flour for dusting

50 ml vegetable oil

90 g butter

40 fresh lambs' kidneys, halved and sinew removed

salt and freshly ground black pepper

Herb-roasted Lambs' Kidneys with Seared Cauliflower

Simmer the red onions in the red wine until the wine has almost completely reduced, then add the meat stock and continue to simmer until the sauce is of a gravy-like consistency.

Cut the cauliflower into 2-cm thick slices, lightly flour them and in batches fry in some of the vegetable oil on each side until lightly coloured.

Add the butter and continue cooking until golden. Keep warm.

Heat a little vegetable oil in a thick-bottomed frying-pan until it is almost smoking, season the kidneys with salt and pepper and fry quickly for a minute or so on each side: they should remain pink inside.

Drain on some kitchen paper.

To serve, put the cauliflower in the centre of each plate, arrange the kidneys on top, then pour the sauce around.

Ask your butcher to bone out your capon for you: it can be a tricky job if you haven't done it before.

You will need to order caul fat (or crépinette) in advance as it is rarely used, these days.

If it's not available, ensure that the bird is well tied.

100 g butter

1 medium onion, peeled and finely chopped

5 g fresh thyme, leaves removed and chopped

400 g boned chicken legs, skinned and minced

100 g fresh white breadcrumbs

1 fresh or tinned black truffle, finely chopped

salt and freshly ground black pepper

1 x 1.5 kg capon or large chicken, boned (save the bones for the stock)

100 g caul fat

vegetable oil for roasting

for the sauce

vegetable oil for frying

1 medium onion, peeled and roughly chopped

2 carrots, peeled and roughly chopped

1 leek, roughly chopped and washed

bones from the capon

2 tbsps plain flour

120 ml red wine

2 ltrs Chicken Stock (see page 35)

a few sprigs of thyme

1 bay leaf

4 cloves garlic, peeled and roughly chopped

Truffle-studded Roast **Capon**

Melt 30 g of the butter in a pan and cook the onion and thyme for a few minutes without colouring.

In a bowl, mix together the minced chicken, breadcrumbs and truffle.

Add the onions, then season with salt and freshly ground pepper.

Lay the boned capon flat on a work surface then arrange the stuffing down the centre.

Roll up the bird overlapping the edges slightly.

Lay out the caul fat and roll the stuffed capon in it a couple of times, then trim the outside edges.

Tie the wrapped capon with string 4–5 times at 6-cm intervals.

Now wrap the whole thing in clingfilm 4–5 times as tightly as it will go.

Put into a large saucepan, cover with cold water, bring to the boil and simmer for 5 minutes.

Remove from the heat, drain off the hot water and leave to cool.

Pre-heat the oven to 200°C/gas mark 6. Heat a roasting-tin large enough for the capon in the oven.

Remove the clingfilm and season the bird.

Add a tablespoon of vegetable oil to the tin and roast the capon for 30–35 minutes, turning and basting occasionally.

Meanwhile, make the sauce.

Heat a little vegetable oil in a thick-bottomed frying-pan and brown the vegetables and chicken bones stirring occasionally.

Dust over the flour and stir well.

Slowly pour in the red wine and chicken stock, mix well, then add the thyme, bay leaf and garlic.

Bring to the boil, skim and simmer gently for an hour, topping up with water if necessary.

Strain the sauce through a fine-meshed sieve then reduce it by boiling rapidly until it has thickened to a gravy-like consistency.

To serve, carve the capon into 1-cm slices.

Large French farmed rabbits are best for this dish. You will probably need to order them in advance from a good butcher.

4 barons good-quality farmed rabbit (the saddle and back legs).

700 ml milk

1 clove garlic, peeled and crushed

1 bay leaf

salt and freshly ground white pepper

70-80 g quick-cooking polenta

100 ml double cream

80 g freshly grated Parmesan

120 ml good veal stock

90 ml extra-virgin olive oil

10 g rosemary, leaves only

60 g stoned good-quality black olives

Grilled Rabbit with Rosemary, Polenta and Black Olives

Remove the fillets from the rabbit saddle, then cut off the legs and, with a sharp knife, remove the thigh bone.

Bring the milk to the boil in a thick-bottomed pan, then add the garlic, bay leaf and seasoning.

Simmer for 5 minutes, then whisk in the polenta.

Turn the heat down as low as it will go and cook slowly for 10 minutes, whisking every so often so that it doesn't stick to the bottom of the pan.

Add the cream and Parmesan and cook for a further 5 minutes.

Pour it into a clean pan, if necessary, cover and put to one side until required.

Reduce the veal stock to a gravy-like consistency.

Pre-heat a charcoal grill, griddle or baking-tray.

Season the rabbit, rub it with a little olive oil and grill the legs first for 6 or 7 minutes on each side until they are just cooked.

Put the fillets on the grill and cook for 1 minute on each side.

Meanwhile, heat the olive oil in a pan, add the rosemary and black olives and cook for a minute or so without colouring.

Reheat the polenta slowly.

Slice the rabbit fillets into three pieces.

To serve, put a spoonful of polenta in the centre of the plate, rest a leg on top, pour a couple of teaspoons of the reduced veal stock around it, arrange the fillets on the plate and spoon over the olives and rosemary.

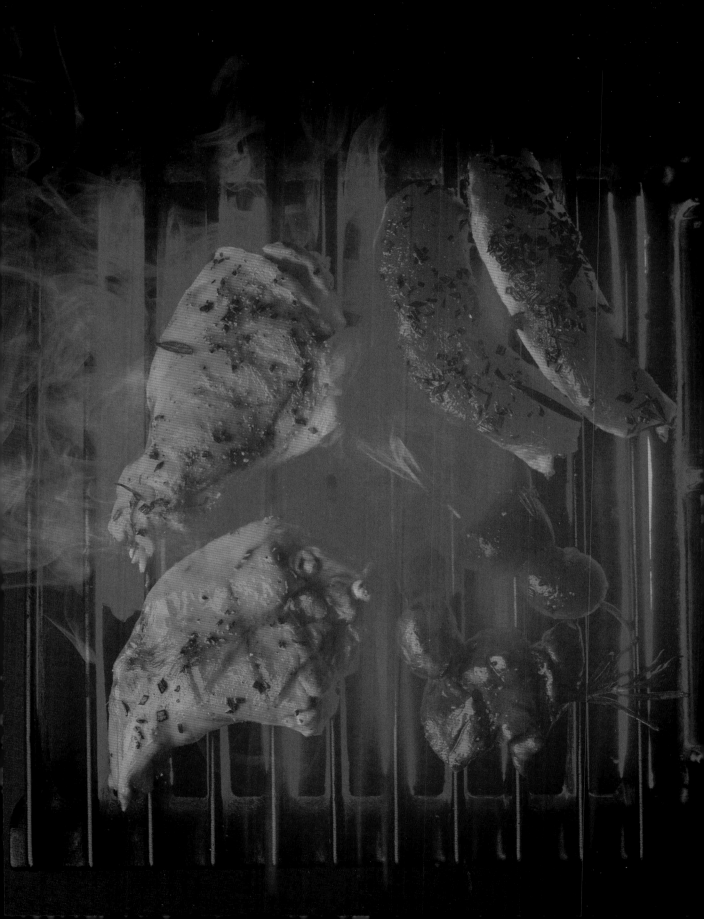

Make this dish in advance as the cooking time is long and a few days in the fridge will only improve the end results.

Various cuts of meat are suited to this dish, but in the restaurant we use a cut called feather fillet, which is not actually fillet but a shoulder muscle. A good alternative is shin of beef or brisket. Avoid buying ready-diced braising beef as this can contain various cuts which will have different cooking times.

8 x 200 g pieces of feather fillet *or* shin of beef *or* flank

3 tbsps plain flour

salt and freshly ground black pepper

vegetable oil for frying

60 g butter

2 onions, peeled and roughly chopped

3 medium carrots, peeled and roughly chopped

4 sticks of celery, roughly chopped

4 cloves garlic, peeled and crushed

5 g thyme, leaves removed and chopped

5 g rosemary, leaves removed and chopped

1 bay leaf

1/2 tbsp tomato purée

250 ml good red wine

750 ml stout or Guinness

1.5 ltrs Dark Meat Stock (see page 34)

cornflour (optional)

for the garnish

5 medium carrots, peeled and thinly sliced on the angle

50 g butter

30 g caster sugar

10 g parsley, washed and finely chopped

Braised **Beef** in Stout

Lightly flour the meat with 1 tablespoon of the flour and season with salt and pepper.

Heat the vegetable oil in a heavy frying-pan and fry the meat on a high heat, a few pieces at a time, until nicely browned.

Heat the butter in a large, heavy-bottomed saucepan and gently fry the onions, carrots, celery and garlic for a few minutes until soft.

Add the thyme, rosemary and bay leaf. Add the flour and tomato purée and stir over a low heat for a minute.

Slowly add the red wine and stout, stirring constantly to avoid lumps forming.

Bring to the boil and simmer until the liquid has reduced by half.

Add the meat stock and the beef, bring back to the boil, cover with a lid and simmer gently for about 2–2 1/2 hours until the meat is tender. It's difficult to put an exact time on braised meats, sometimes an extra half-an-hour may be required depending on the meat itself. The best way to check is by actually tasting the meat.

Once the meat is cooked the sauce should have thickened sufficiently, but if not, dilute a little cornflour in some water and stir into the sauce and simmer for a few minutes.

Put the carrots into a pan and just cover them with water, add the butter, the caster sugar and salt and freshly ground black pepper.

Bring to the boil and simmer gently for about 15 minutes until the liquid has almost evaporated and the carrots are tender.

Drain any excess liquid from the carrots and stir in the parsley.

Serve the pieces of beef on individual plates or on a large serving dish with the sauce poured over and carrots scattered on top.

A good accompaniment would be mashed parsnip or potato.

2 kg good-quality, coarsely minced beef (preferably rib mince), including 20 per cent fat

10 onions, peeled, halved and thinly sliced

60 ml vegetable oil, plus a little extra

salt and freshly ground black pepper

60 g butter

for the sauce

1 onion, peeled and finely chopped

30 ml olive oil

1 tbsp tomato purée

1 x 250 g tin chopped tomatoes

salt and freshly ground black pepper

2 tbsps American mustard

4 tbsps tomato ketchup

Chopped **Steak** Americain

Mould the beef into 8 even-sized balls, then flatten them and refrigerate until required.

Cook the onions in the vegetable oil over a low heat in a covered pan.

Remove the lid, season with salt and pepper, add the butter and turn up the heat a little.

Allow the onions to colour and, once golden, remove from the heat and put to one side.

Meanwhile, make the sauce. Sweat the onion in the olive oil until soft, add the tomato purée and chopped tomatoes, bring it to the boil, season with salt and pepper and simmer for 25–30 minutes.

Remove from the heat and leave to cool.

Then mix in the mustard and tomato ketchup.

A barbecue or charcoal grill is ideal for cooking the chopped steaks.

Alternatively pre-heat a grill to maximum, lightly oil and season the chopped steaks with salt and pepper, then grill them for about 3–4 minutes on each side for medium rare or more or less as preferred.

Serve with the hot onions and the sauce at room temperature.

Fish have always been mystical, have had a special place at the table. However familiar a battered cod may seem, a fresh cod on a slab, slimy and cold, mouth gaping, is as different from us and our atmosphere and our world as it is possible to be.

Two-thirds of the world is water, three-quarters of us is water, but fish are utterly, truly alien. We have a reverence and a repugnance of things that drown in our atmosphere. The measure of human inquisitiveness and bravery is measured against the first man who ever ate an oyster. Fish are sinister. Deep-sea fishing is more closely related to space travel than it is to terrestrial hunting or farming. Alone in a fatal environment, fishermen navigate by the stars and their catch is always a mysterious act of faith. Indeed fishing over the other side of the boat was one of the first Christian acts of faith. You drop a net and out of the deep comes these aliens. In the case of turbot, literally, flat fish are born round fish, and slowly one eye grows over to join the other, sometimes it's the left, sometimes the right. Turbot are sinister. Plaice are dextrous without having the benefit of hands. The salmon was the ancient Celtic symbol of wisdom. The fish was the first symbol of Christ.

The French have an aphorism that fish must swim three times – once in water, once in wine and once in butter – but when you confront it on the plate, luke cool, fat-free brain food, healthy size-ten light lunch, remember that in all its life, the fish had no idea, no inkling that you ever existed, that there was any world but water and moon magnet's face. Everything else we eat, we share a life with, in a field, a wood, a pen, a coop, a window box, a cloche, a furrow. They know us and we know them, but not fish. Not in a fish's wildest dreams are we real. We are the true extra-terrestrials, and when you think about that, it's five fathoms deeply weird.

Le Caprice is one of the few restaurants where I regularly make fish a first choice. While a lot of the customers might imagine fish as vegetables and be exercising their feminine sides, the kitchen sensibly takes a robustly Ahab line on fish and serves it up with a gutsy respect. There is none of that precious little precious little and none of the damp origami or the drizzled, seared, slabbo, anonymous meat, fish that swims untasted and unremembered through so many lunch times. Le Caprice has never lost sight of the newspaper heritage of its raw ingredients and will serve the posh and the prole with the same care.

I particularly commend the razor clams to you, not the easiest of ingredients to find, but worth remembering you've got this recipe if you do. The Jerusalem artichoke mash is one of the best accompaniments for a sea bass, a fish that has been paired off with more unsuitable partners than Elizabeth Taylor. As a general rule, if fish comes with more than two attendants, the whole thing will detract from the star ingredient

Razor clams are not often seen on the fishmonger's slab.

The idea came from a meal in Spain, where they were cooked very simply; and that's the only way to prepare these phallic-looking objects.

2 kg live razor clams

50 ml white wine

10 g thyme

3 cloves garlic, peeled and roughly chopped

1 small onion, peeled and roughly chopped

2 tsps salt
stalks from the parsley (see below)

120 g butter

for the parsley crust:

90 g butter

4 cloves garlic, peeled and crushed

15 g parsley, stalks removed and reserved, washed and finely chopped

60 g fresh white breadcrumbs

salt and freshly ground black pepper

Baked **Razor Clams**
with Parsley and Garlic

Carefully wash the razor clams in cold running water for 10 minutes.

Put them into a saucepan with the white wine, thyme, garlic, onion, salt and parsley stalks, cover with a lid and cook on a high heat for a few minutes, giving the occasional stir, until all the shells open.

Drain in a colander, reserve the liquid, and leave to cool.

To make the parsley crust, melt the butter in a pan and gently cook the garlic for a minute.

Stir in the parsley and breadcrumbs and season with salt and pepper.

Pre-heat the grill to maximum temperature.

Carefully remove the clams from their shells, keeping their shells intact.

Cut away the dark-looking sacs and discard them.

Cut each clam into 4–5 pieces and lay them back in the shells.

Lay the shells on a grill-pan, scatter them with the parsley crust and brown under the grill for 4–5 minutes.

Meanwhile, strain the cooking liquid, bring back to the boil, whisk in the butter and spoon around the clams.

650 g dry mashed potato (with no butter or milk added)

650 g salmon fillet, poached in fish stock and flaked

2 tbsps tomato ketchup

2 tsps anchovy essence

3 tsps English mustard

salt and freshly ground white pepper

for the sauce

1/2 ltr strong Fish Stock (see page 35)

50 g butter

30 g flour

50 ml white wine

250 ml double cream

15 g fresh sorrel, shredded

salt and freshly ground white pepper

1.5 kg spinach, picked over, washed and dried

Salmon **Fishcakes** with Sorrel Sauce

To make the fishcakes, mix together the potato, half of the poached salmon, the ketchup, anchovy essence, mustard and seasoning until it is smooth.

Fold in the remaining salmon.

Mould the mixture into 8 round cakes and refrigerate.

To make the sauce, bring the fish stock to the boil in a thick-bottomed pan.

In another pan, melt the butter and stir in the flour.

Cook very slowly over a low heat for 30 seconds, then gradually whisk in the fish stock.

Pour in the white wine and simmer for 30 minutes until the sauce has thickened.

Add the cream and reduce the sauce until it is of a thick, pouring consistency, then put in

the sorrel and season. Preheat the oven to 200°C/gas mark 6.

Lightly flour the fishcakes and fry them until they are coloured on both sides, then bake for 10–15 minutes.

Heat a large saucepan over a medium flame, add the spinach, no extra water, season lightly with salt and pepper and cover it tightly with a lid.

Cook for 3–4 minutes, stirring occasionally, until the leaves are tender. Drain well in a colander.

To serve, put some spinach on each plate, then a fishcake and pour over the sauce.

Eat immediately.

1.5 kg Jerusalem
artichokes, peeled

5 g rosemary,
leaves removed

2 cloves garlic, peeled
and roughly chopped

60 ml extra-virgin olive
oil, plus a little extra

salt and freshly ground
black pepper

1.5 kg sea bass fillet,
scaled, trimmed and
bones removed

90 g butter

flour for dusting

Fillet of **Sea Bass**
with Jerusalem
Artichoke Mash

Put the Jerusalem
artichokes into a pan
with the rosemary, garlic
and olive oil, just cover
with cold water and
season with salt and
pepper.

Bring to the boil and
cook on a medium heat
for about 15 minutes
until the artichokes are
soft, almost falling apart,
and the liquid has nearly
evaporated.

If there is still a lot of
liquid left, turn up the
heat to evaporate it.

Take the artichokes off
the heat and mash
them.

The texture should be
relatively coarse. If it
seems a little wet, put it
back on a medium heat
stirring occasionally.

Leave on one side and
keep warm.

Cut the sea bass into
even-sized portions,
then season it with salt
and pepper.

Lightly flour the skin
side. Heat the butter in a
heavy frying-pan and fry
the bass, skin side down
first, for 3–4 minutes on
each side, getting the
skin as crisp as
possible.

If you are cooking for a
large number, fry all of the
fish briefly then put it on a
baking-sheet and finish it
in a hot oven for a few
minutes just before
serving.

Serve the sea bass with a
spoonful of the artichoke
mash and drizzle over
some extra-virgin olive oil.

Buying scallops off the shelf can be difficult: they often look great but when cooked will shed water because they have been overwashed or soaked in water, which they take in like a sponge. Try to get your fishmonger to cut and trim your scallops fresh from the shell, and wash them only briefly.

Allow 5 or 6 medium-sized scallops per person, or more if they are smaller.

for the mousseline potato

1.5 kg large floury potatoes, peeled and cut into even-sized pieces

150 ml double cream

150 ml milk

salt and freshly ground white pepper

100 g butter

100 ml extra-virgin olive oil

enough scallops for 8 people

salt and freshly ground black pepper

30 ml olive oil

250 g butter

2 cloves garlic, peeled and crushed (more if you wish)

10 g parsley, washed and finely chopped

juice of 1 lemon

Griddled **Scallops** with Mousseline Potato

Cook the potatoes in boiling salted water, drain them in a colander then return to the pan on a low heat for a minute to evaporate any excess water.

Purée them in a food-processor until smooth with the cream and milk, season with salt and pepper, then slowly add the butter and olive oil to the machine while it's still running until the potato is creamy and light: it should be of a stiff pouring consistency.

Transfer to a saucepan and keep warm.

Season the scallops with salt and pepper.

Get a heavy-bottomed frying-pan hot until almost smoking (hope your extraction fan is good!), rub the bottom with a little olive oil and cook the scallops for about 1 minute on each side, giving them a nice caramel colour.

In another pan while the scallops are cooking get the butter foaming then add the garlic, parsley and lemon juice.

Remove the pan from the heat.

Put a couple of spoonfuls of the potato in the middle of each plate, arrange the scallops around it then spoon the hot butter over the scallops.

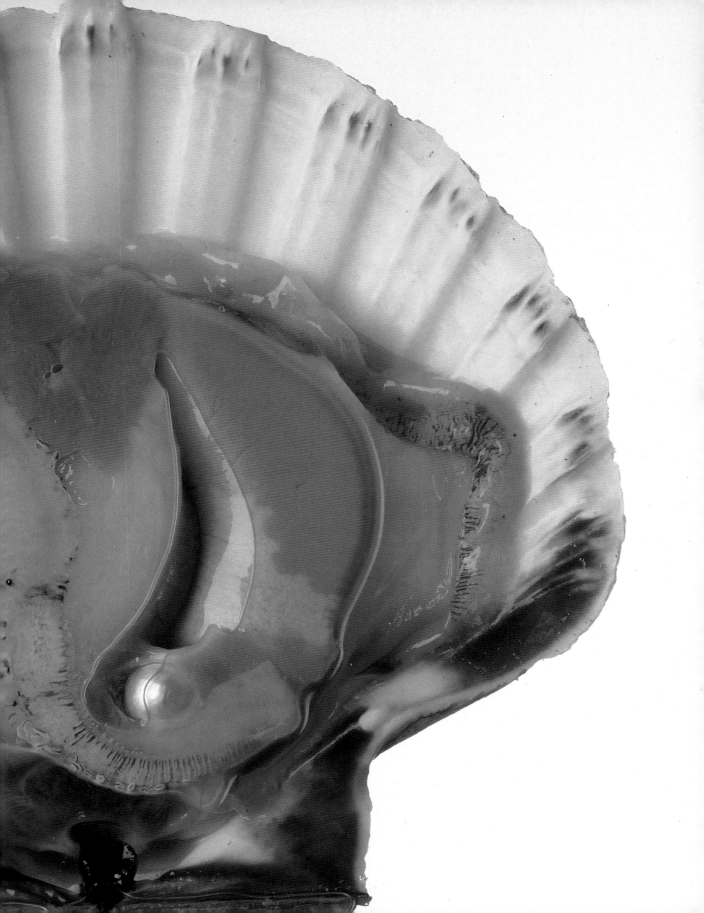

Griddled Scallops with Mousseline Potato

A perfect dish to serve from the barbecue or as a light quick lunch or dinner-party dish.

Ask your fishmonger to clean the squid for you, leaving the body tubes whole and cutting the tentacles just above the eyes so that they stay intact.

for the chilli salsa

90 ml extra-virgin olive oil

1 medium-sized mild chilli, seeded and finely chopped

2 red peppers, seeded and finely chopped

zest of 1 lime, finely grated

1 tbsp sweet chilli sauce

10 g mint, leaves removed and finely chopped

salt and freshly ground black pepper

8 medium-sized squid, weighing about 400 g each

vegetable oil

16 rashers thinly sliced pancetta or smoked streaky bacon

250 g rocket, wild preferably

Char-grilled Squid
with Italian Bacon

To make the chilli salsa, heat the olive oil in a pan and gently cook the chilli, the peppers and the lime zest for a few minutes until soft.

Remove from the heat and stir in the chilli sauce and mint.

Season with salt and pepper and put to one side.

Preheat a barbecue, griddle or cast-iron frying-pan.

Make a cut down the centre of the squid and open it out flat.

Season it and the tentacles with salt and pepper and smear lightly with vegetable oil.

Meanwhile, grill the bacon until crisp.

Cook the squid for 2–3 minutes on each side, then serve with a pile of the rocket and a spoonful of the warm salsa with the bacon on top.

Lobster Salad with Crushed Potatoes and Alsace Bacon.

1.5 kg salmon fillet, skinned, trimmed and bones removed

salt and freshly ground black pepper

10 g chervil, finely chopped

5 g dill, finely chopped

10 g parsley, finely chopped

120 ml extra-virgin olive oil

2 cucumbers, peeled

350–400 g asparagus tips, cooked in boiling salted water for 3 minutes until tender

250 g good-quality mayonnaise

for the dressing

20 ml red wine vinegar

100 ml extra-virgin olive oil

1/2 tsp caster sugar

salt and freshly ground black pepper

Herb-roasted
Salmon Mayonnaise
with Peppered Cucumber and Asparagus

Pre-heat the oven to 240°C/gas mark 9.

Cut the salmon into even-sized portions and season lightly with salt and pepper.

Mix together the chopped herbs and dip one side of the salmon into them.

Heat about 60 ml of the olive oil in a roasting-tray in the oven until it is almost smoking.

Put the pieces of salmon in, herb side down first, and cook for about 3 minutes on each side.

Remove from the oven and leave to cool.

Cut the cucumbers in half lengthways and carefully scrape out the seeds with a teaspoon.

Holding the knife at a 45° angle, cut the cucumber into 2-cm-thick slices.

Adjust your peppermill to a coarse grind and heavily season the slices of cucumber.

Heat the rest of the olive oil in a frying-pan and sauté the cucumber a few slices at a time for 2–3 minutes until they are a nice golden colour (the pan will need to be very hot or the cucumber will boil).

Put them to one side. Make the dressing by whisking together all the ingredients.

To serve, arrange the cucumber on a plate with the salmon on top.

Dress the asparagus with the vinaigrette and scatter it over the salmon.

Either serve the mayonnaise on the plate or pass it round separately.

1 bay leaf

5 g thyme

1 tsp black peppercorns

1 onion, peeled and roughly chopped

1 tsp fennel seeds

1 tbsp sea salt

8 small live 450 g, or 4 large 1 kg lobsters or buy them ready-cooked

700–800 g good-flavoured large new potatoes, peeled, cooked and kept warm

100 g good-quality mayonnaise

1 tsp Dijon mustard

8–10 g chervil, roughly chopped

24 thinly sliced rashers smoked streaky bacon

100–120 g small salad leaves (corn salad, landcress, rocket, etc.)

10 g fine chives, cut into 5-cm lengths

for the dressing

1 small carrot, peeled and finely chopped

2 shallots, peeled and finely chopped

1 clove garlic, peeled and crushed

40 g root ginger, scraped and finely chopped

50 ml dark soy sauce

30 ml white wine vinegar

2 tbsps tomato ketchup

150 ml sunflower or vegetable oil

5 g coriander leaves, washed and finely chopped

salt and freshly ground black pepper

Lobster Salad with Crushed Potatoes and Alsace Bacon

You may need to cook the lobsters in 2 batches unless you have a very large pan.

Half fill a large pan with water, add the bay leaf, thyme, peppercorns, onion, fennel seeds and salt.

Bring to the boil and simmer for 15 minutes.

Add the lobsters to the water.

Cook small ones for 8–10 minutes and larger ones for 12–15 minutes.

Remove them from the water and leave to cool.

To make the dressing, mix the carrot, shallots, garlic and ginger with the soy sauce, rice vinegar and ketchup.

Gradually whisk in the oil, stir in the coriander and season to taste.

While the potatoes are still warm, mash them coarsely with a fork or masher, then mix in the mayonnaise, mustard and chervil and put to one side.

Remove the lobster meat from the bodies and claws and cut into even-sized pieces.

Meanwhile grill the bacon rashers until crisp.

To serve, put a couple of spoonfuls of the potato salad in the middle of a plate, arrange the salad leaves around it and lightly spoon over the dressing.

Place the lobster pieces on the potato and the bacon on top, then scatter over the chives.

Cooking **Fish** Whole

The thought of serving fish on the bone is enough for most not to even entertain the idea. Even though the flavour and moisture is retained, it is worth scraping around the bones for. This type of cooking method should be used with firmer fleshed fish, such as sea bass, snapper, grouper and dorade which also have less bones to contend with. Serving a whole fish for 6–8 people can look very impressive stuffed with whole herbs and garlic cloves or dried fennel sticks.

Try scoring the flesh and inserting sliced limes or lemons or rubbing spices into the skin before roasting.

Ask your fishmonger to scale the fish, cut the fins off and remove the stomach. The head can be left on or removed depending on how squeamish you are.

When cooking whole fish on the bone allow about 40 minutes per kilo and cook in a hot oven or on the barbecue for smaller individual fish. Serve as simply as possible, i.e. with a salad, simply cooked potatoes and a light butter- or oil-based sauce.

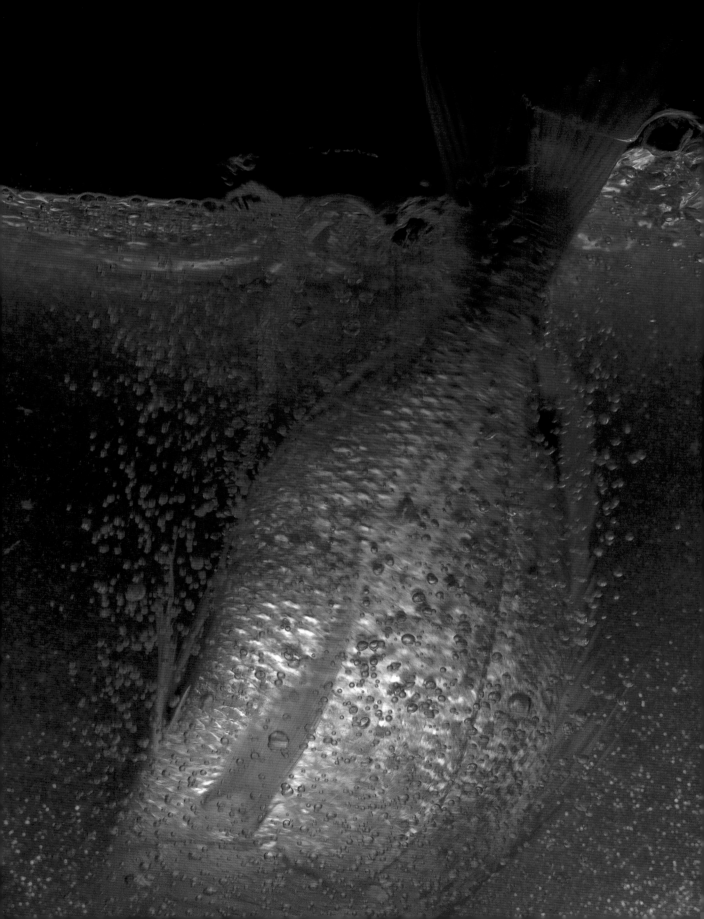

Vegetables

Creamed **Celeriac**

Celeriac, like most root vegetables, is very versatile and lends itself to roasting, boiling and puréeing.

Creamed celeriac will go with most meats, game and simply grilled fish.

1.5 kg celeriac, peeled and cut into even-sized pieces

salt and freshly ground black pepper

60 ml double cream

60 g butter

1 tsp celery salt

Put the celeriac into a saucepan, cover it with cold water and a teaspoon of salt.

Bring it to the boil and simmer for 15–20 minutes.

Drain it into a colander, then return to the pan on a low heat for 1 minute to allow any excess water to evaporate.

Blend the celeriac in a food-processor until it is smooth.

Return it to a clean pan, stir in the cream and butter over a low heat and season with pepper and celery salt.

Parmesan-baked **Marrow** with Wild Garlic

Marrow need not be seen as a boring English vegetable. It is a large courgette, which we seem to forget, and should be treated in the same way.

Wild garlic is available from the end of February for a couple of months. If unavailable, replace it with ordinary garlic cloves.

1.5 kg marrow

90 ml olive oil

1 large onion, peeled and finely chopped

60 g wild garlic leaves, roughly chopped or 3 cloves garlic, peeled and crushed

10 g thyme, leaves removed and chopped

10 plum tomatoes, peeled and seeded

salt and freshly ground black pepper

120 g freshly grated Parmesan

If the skin seems tough peel the marrow.

Cut it into 4 lengthways, scoop out the seeds then cut it into 2-cm-thick slices.

Heat half of the olive oil in a heavy frying-pan and fry the marrow for 4–5 minutes until golden, then put it to one side.

Heat the rest of the olive oil in the same pan and fry the onion, garlic and thyme, without colouring, until they are soft.

Add the tomatoes, season with salt and pepper and return the marrow to the pan.

Pre-heat the oven to 230°C/gas mark 8.

Put the marrow into a heatproof dish, scatter it with the Parmesan and bake for 15–20 minutes until golden.

Caramelised Endive with Capers and Lemon

This dish makes a good, simple starter or an accompaniment to roast meats and game.

8 large heads of Belgian endives (chicory)

60 g caster sugar

juice of 1 lemon

salt and freshly ground black pepper

30 ml vegetable oil

90 g butter

60 g capers, drained

2 lemons, segmented and cut into small pieces

Trim any discoloured leaves from the endives and put them into a saucepan with 30 g of the sugar, the lemon juice and 2 teaspoons of salt.

Cover with water, bring to the boil, put on the lid and simmer for 20 minutes.

Remove from the water with a slotted spoon and drain on some kitchen paper.

Pre-heat the oven to 200°C/gas mark 6. Heat the vegetable oil in a large frying-pan.

Season the endives, then gently fry them until they are a light golden colour.

Add the butter and sprinkle over the rest of the sugar.

Stir well and transfer to an ovenproof dish.

Bake for 15–20 minutes, giving them the occasional stir.

Remove from the oven, sprinkle over the capers and lemons, stir well and serve.

Cumin-roasted Carrots

Roasting carrots changes the nature of this humble vegetable, concentrating the flavour and bringing out the natural sweetness.

Serve with almost any main course or at room temperature with cold meats.

1.5 kg medium carrots, trimmed and peeled

30 ml olive oil

salt and freshly ground black pepper

1 tsp ground cumin

1 tsp cumin seeds

60 g butter

10 g parsley, washed and finely chopped

Pre-heat the oven to 200°C/gas mark 6.

Slice the carrots about 1/2 cm thick at an angle.

Heat the olive oil in a thick-bottomed frying-pan and gently cook the carrots until they turn a light golden colour.

Season with salt and pepper, add the ground cumin and the cumin seeds and turn the mixture into an ovenproof dish.

Bake for 20–25 minutes, giving the occasional stir until the carrots are cooked through and a nice golden colour.

Add the butter and parsley, stir well and serve immediately.

Creamed Brussels **Sprouts**

A good alternative to buttered Brussels sprouts, and a perfect accompaniment to game and poultry.

1 kg large Brussels sprouts, prepared and cooked

200 ml double cream

salt and freshly ground black pepper

60 g butter

Slice the sprouts thinly.

Pour the cream into a pan and reduce it by half, then add the sprouts and season with salt and pepper.

Simmer for 4–5 minutes on a low heat, stirring every so often.

Add the butter and serve.

Squash and pumpkins vary in shape and size, and butternut is probably one of the easiest to prepare.

It also has the most consistent flavour. New types of squash appear all the time on supermarket shelves and normally carry cooking instructions on them.

Serve with grilled fish, poultry or with a selection of other starters.

for the tomato and coriander relish

2 large shallots, peeled and finely chopped

50 ml balsamic vinegar

300 g plum tomatoes, peeled, seeded and cut into rough 1-cm dice

10 g coriander, finely chopped

100 ml extra-virgin olive oil

salt and freshly ground black pepper

1.5 kg squash or pumpkin, peeled, if necessary, and cut into even-sized pieces

60 ml olive oil

Roasted Squash with Tomato and Coriander Relish

Pre-heat the oven to 220°C/gas mark 7.

First, make the tomato and coriander relish.

Simmer the shallots in the balsamic vinegar for a couple of minutes until the vinegar has almost completely reduced.

Remove from the heat and transfer to a mixing bowl.

Add the other ingredients, stir well and season to taste.

Heat the olive oil in a roasting tin in the oven.

Put in the squash, season it with salt and pepper, then cook for 20–30 minutes, stirring occasionally.

Serve topped with the tomato relish.

Deep-fried Hash Browns

2 medium onions,
peeled and thinly sliced

30 g butter

1 kg large potatoes,
cooked in their skins,
peeled and grated

1 egg white, half beaten

200 g dry mashed
potato

50 g potato flour

1/2 tsp celery salt

salt and freshly ground
black pepper

good vegetable oil for
deep-frying

Heat the butter in a pan
and cook the onions
slowly until they are soft.

Put the onions into a
bowl, add the grated
potato and mix them
together with the egg
white.

Stir in the mashed potato,
the potato flour, celery
salt and seasoning.

If the mixture is a little wet,
add more potato flour.

Pre-heat a deep-fat fryer
to 170°C with 8 cm of oil.

Test the mixture by rolling
a couple of little balls of it
in the palm of your hand
and dropping them into
the hot fat.

When they are cooked,
taste them and, if
necessary, adjust the
seasoning.

Then roll the rest into
walnut-sized balls and
cook them in batches.

Note: You can half fry the
Hash Browns in advance,
then crisp them up in hot
fat before you serve them.

Le Caprice

Cheese: Melted Tallegio with Baked Plum Tomatoes and Foccacia 5.50

Dessert: Pannacotta with Raspberries   5.75
         Minted Chocolate Chip Ice Cream   5.25
         Cherry Pie with Sour Cream   5.50
         Sherry Trifle with Summer Fruits   5.75
         Banana Sticky Toffee Pudding   6.00
         Cappuccino Brûlé   6.25
         Baked Alaska   6.25
         Blackberry Summer Pudding   6.50
         Elderflower Jelly with Summer Fruits   6.50
         Double Chocolate Pudding Soufflé   6.75
         Scandinavian Iced Berries with White Chocolate Sauce 6.75
         Eton Mess with Wild Strawberries   9.50

         Chocolate Truffles   2.00
         Chocolate Chip Cookies and Brownies   4.00

Coffee: Ethiopian Full Roast
         Filter   2.50
         Espresso   small   2.25
                                               large   2.75
         Cappuccino   3.00
         Fresh ground decaffeinated coffee available
         Hot Chocolate   2.75

         Selection Fauchon
Tea: Darjeeling, Camomile, Mint, Jasmine or Verveine   2.00

We ask smokers to show consideration for other diners

Desserts

Desserts

Dessert

The last course, unless you're going for savouries, should be called pudding. It's pudding because the unassailable home of puddings is here in England. No other cuisine comes close to our heritage of sweet things. The French rather despise puddings, thinking of them as being an offshoot of millinery and a separate breed of chef confectioners make them. They are also responsible for ice sculpture. In Italy they're all unashamedly infantile and sloppy. Only in Germany is our pre-eminence challenged but it's not close, not really. English puddings are the soul of our cooking.

The word itself is English, not a French derivative like dessert. It comes with solid shire directness from the word for an animal's stomach. Only in the last few years has pudding been consigned to sweet things and custard (*la crème anglaise*) suet puddings, steak and kidney puddings, beef and oyster puddings. You could eat nothing but pudding in England. Now you'll eat everything but, as meals become ever more truncated so pudding goes from being an optional extra to a sort of mild eccentricity, eschewed by most, but rather than disappear from menus pudding remains as a sort of dare. Pudding is brave, it's raffish, it's optimistic and let me tell you, pudding is also an aphrodisiac.

Now, I haven't mentioned aphrodisiacs up until now because they're all bollocks and there's nothing so boring than people who think they can make up for a lack of charm and sex appeal by taking on the souls of half-a-dozen bivales, but pudding is a true aphrodisiac in the sense that it is a libidinous post-it note, a promise of sweetmeats to come. Frankly if I were on a first date (and it's such a long time ago since I had a first date) with a girl who didn't eat pudding, there wouldn't be a second date. No matter what her appurtenances and attractions, it would all end in dreariness. Pudding is what separates the truly erotically sybaritic from those who only read articles about the erotically sybaritic. Pudding is for people who live comfortably in their skins, who like who they are, who would like you to like who they are, not who they may turn into if they do enough bits of corporeal manipulation, wear the right underwear and get their hair cut by a man who appears in magazines. Pudding promises laughter and high expectations and good humour.

If you don't have an appetite for food, do you have an appetite for anything? And if you don't have an appetite for pudding, do you really have an appetite or appreciation for food?

The meringue is the most time-consuming part of this dish, so make it a day or two before you need it, or cheat and buy some good-quality meringue from a baker or supermarket.

for the meringue

2 egg whites

120 g caster sugar

to serve

200 g strawberries, hulled

750 ml double cream

100 g caster sugar

1 tsp vanilla essence

150 g wild strawberries, or more if you're feeling indulgent

To make the meringue, whisk the egg whites until very stiff, then gradually add the caster sugar until it forms peaks when the whisk is removed. An electric mixer will give the best results.

Spread the meringue on a baking-tray lined with greaseproof paper and place it in the oven at the lowest temperature setting.

Bake overnight until it is dry and brittle.

Process the strawberries in a blender until smooth. Whip the cream, the 100 g caster sugar and the vanilla essence together until stiff.

Break the meringue into small pieces and fold it into the cream with half of the strawberry purée.

To serve, spoon the cream mixture into the middle of the plate, then drizzle some of the strawberry purée around the outside and scatter the wild strawberries over the top.

Eton Mess with
Wild Strawberries

500 g red cherries or
good-quality canned
black cherries, stoned

200 g caster sugar

100 ml water

2 tsps arrowroot or
cornflour

500 g puff pastry

softened butter

1 egg, beaten

icing sugar for dusting

250 g sour cream or
crème fraîche

Cherry Pie with Sour Cream

Put the cherries in
a saucepan with the
caster sugar and water.

Bring to the boil
and simmer for 5
minutes.
(If using canned
cherries replace the
water and sugar
with the syrup from
the can.)

Dilute the arrowroot with
a little water, add to the
cherries and simmer for
a further 3–4 minutes,
stirring occasionally.

Transfer into a bowl, lay a
piece of clingfilm on the
surface of the cherries to
prevent a skin forming
and leave to cool.

Roll out the puff pastry
on a floured table to
about 2 mm thick.

Cut 8 discs large enough
to line individual 8–10 cm
tart tins leaving 1 cm
of pastry overlapping the
edge.

Cut 8 more discs to fit
the tops. Lightly grease
the tins with butter and
line them with the larger
pastry discs.

Spoon in the cherries,
fold the edge over, brush
with the beaten egg, then
press on the top disc.

Leave to rest in the fridge
for 1 hour.

Brush again with more
egg, then bake the pies
on a tray for 20–25
minutes until golden.

Serve dusted with icing
sugar and a generous
spoonful of the sour
cream.

for the sablé pastry

185 g unsalted butter

225 g icing sugar

3 egg yolks

300 g plain flour (plus a little extra for dusting)

for the filling

450 g golden syrup

100 g dark treacle

450 ml double cream

150 g oatmeal

4 eggs, beaten

juice of ¹/₂ lemon

Treacle Tart

First make the pastry. In a food-processor, mixer or by hand, cream together the butter and icing sugar until they are light and fluffy.

Add the egg yolks, mix well, then fold in the flour. Press the dough into a ball and refrigerate it for a couple of hours.

On a floured table, roll out the pastry to about 1/2 cm thick.

Grease and line a 22–24 cm x 4–5 cm deep flan ring and line it with the pastry.

Leave to rest in the fridge for 1 hour.

Pre-heat the oven to 160°C /gas mark 3.

Meanwhile mix together the golden syrup, treacle, cream, oatmeal and eggs, then stir in the lemon juice.

Don't be alarmed if this looks very runny.

Fill the tart and bake for 40–50 minutes, then remove from the oven and leave to cool.

Serve warm with some thick cream.

Chocolate **Brownie**

250 g unsalted butter, melted

70 g cocoa powder

110 g good-quality dark chocolate, melted

5 eggs, beaten

500 g caster sugar

70 g strong plain flour

70 g soft plain flour

1 tsp baking powder

110 g walnuts, chopped

Pre-heat the oven to 180°C/gas mark 4.

Mix the butter, cocoa powder and melted chocolate together.

In a food-processor or mixer, or by hand, whisk together the eggs and caster sugar until they are light and fluffy.

Sieve together the flours and baking powder, then carefully fold them into the egg mixture with the melted chocolate and the chopped walnuts.

Line a deep baking-tray with buttered greaseproof paper, pour in the mixture and bake for 25–30 minutes.

Once cooked the brownie will still be soft in the centre.

Leave to rest in the baking-tray for an hour or so before turning out and cutting.

Chocolate Chip **Cookies**

100 g unsalted butter

60 g light brown sugar

1 egg, beaten

1/2 tsp baking powder

a few drops of vanilla essence

150 g plain flour

100 g good-quality dark or milk chocolate buttons

150–200 g good-quality dark or milk chocolate for dipping

Cream together the butter and sugar in a food-processor, or by hand, until light and fluffy.

Slowly add the egg, ensuring you scrape the sides of the food-processor bowl.

Turn the mixture into a bowl and carefully fold in the baking powder, vanilla essence, flour and chocolate buttons and mix well.

Rest in the fridge for 30 minutes or so until the mixture is pliable but not solid.

Place the dough on a sheet of clingfilm and roll it into a large sausage shape, then wrap it and refrigerate it for an hour or so until firm.

Pre-heat the oven to 175°C/gas mark 4.

Cut the cookie dough into 2 1/2-cm-thick slices and lay them on a baking sheet.

Bake for 8–10 minutes until they are a light golden colour (they should still be a little soft to touch).

Remove to a cake rack and leave to cool.

Melt the chocolate in a bain-marie or in a bowl over a pan of simmering water.

Dip one side of each cookie into the chocolate, then leave in the refrigerator to set, chocolate side down, on a tray covered with clingfilm or greaseproof paper.

for the toffee sauce

640 ml double cream

340 g caster sugar

130 g glucose (optional)

130 g unsalted butter

for the sponge

450 g strong plain flour

10 g baking powder

3 g bicarbonate of soda

130 g unsalted butter (removed from fridge)

375 g light brown sugar

3 medium eggs, lightly beaten

4 bananas, peeled and mashed

Banana Sticky Toffee Pudding

Pre-heat the oven to 175°C/gas mark 4.

To make the toffee sauce, pour half of the cream and the other ingredients into a thick-bottomed pan and mix well.

Bring it to the boil, stirring with a wooden spoon, and continue to boil until it is golden brown.

Remove the sauce from the heat, allow it to cool slightly, then whisk in the remaining cream.

Grease and line a baking-tin, measuring approximately 30 cm x 24 cm x 6 cm deep, with greaseproof paper.

Now make the sponge.

Sift together the flour, baking powder and bicarbonate of soda.

In a food-processor or mixer, cream the butter and sugar on a medium speed until it is light and fluffy.

Add the eggs slowly, taking care that the mixture does not separate. (If this does happen, add a little of the flour and continue mixing for a minute or so.)

Then fold in the sifted flour slowly until it is smooth.

Finally, stir in the mashed bananas.

Spread the mixture in the baking-tin and bake for 50–60 minutes or until the sponge is firm to the touch.

Allow it to cool – it can be left in the tin.

Remove the cake from the tin and trim the outside edges.

Cut it horizontally into three then reassemble it in the baking-tin, spreading two-thirds of the sauce between the layers.

Once you have assembled the pudding, reheat it in the oven at 175°C/gas mark 4 for 15–20 minutes.

Then cut it into 8 equal servings and top it with the remaining toffee sauce.

Serve it with ice cream, soured cream or crème fraîche.

Pancakes

Basic Pancake Batter
serves 6–8
(makes approximately
24 pancakes)

120 g flour

1 medium egg

1 tsp caster sugar, for
sweet fillings

250 ml milk

vegetable oil for frying

Whisk together the flour,
egg and sugar (if using)
with a third of the milk
until smooth.

Then whisk in the
remaining milk and strain
if necessary.

Heat a non-stick frying-
pan or a favourite
alternative pan, rub it
with a little vegetable oil
then pour in some
pancake mix.

Tilt the pan immediately
so that the mixture
spreads evenly.

Turn after a minute with
a spatula or palette knife.

Remove from the pan
and keep warm while
you cook the rest.

If you want to make a
large quantity of
pancakes, make them in
advance and stack them
between squares of
greaseproof paper.

Reheat them in the oven
for a minute or so before
serving.

Alternatively the batter
will keep in the fridge for
up to 2 days, then rewhisk
before use.

American Pancakes with Maple Syrup

175 ml milk

5 g fresh yeast

1 tsp vegetable oil

a pinch of salt

1 egg yolk

10 g caster sugar

110 g plain flour

120 ml maple syrup

Warm the milk until it is
tepid, remove it from the
heat then add the yeast
and stir until it has
dissolved.

Add the oil, salt, egg
yolk, sugar and flour,
and mix well to make
a smooth batter.

Cover and leave in
a warm place for 30
minutes until it begins
to ferment, when
bubbles will appear
on top of the mixture.

Heat a non-stick or
heavy frying-pan, rub it
with a little vegetable oil
then pour in 2
tablespoons of batter.

Turn the pancake after
about a minute and cook
on the other side.

Once cooked they can be
stored on a tray and
reheated in the oven at
200°C/gas mark 6 for two
or three minutes.

Serve on warm plates
with a generous pouring
of maple syrup.

for the pancakes

400 g ricotta

350 ml milk

8 eggs, separated

300 g plain flour

3 tsps baking powder

a good pinch of salt

butter for cooking

to serve

400 g Greek yoghurt

250–300 g blueberries

200 g clear honey

Ricotta Pancakes with Blueberries and Greek Yoghurt

Gently whisk together the ricotta, the milk and the egg yolks.

Sift together the flour and the baking powder, then fold into the ricotta mix with the salt.

Whisk the egg whites in a separate bowl until they form stiff peaks.

Fold them into the batter with a large spoon.

Cover and leave in the fridge for an hour or so.

To cook the pancakes, melt a little butter in a non-stick pan, then wipe it out with some kitchen paper.

Drop in a couple of tablespoons of the batter to form a rough 10-cm pancake.

Fry on a low heat for a couple of minutes on each side until just cooked, then transfer the pancake on to greaseproof paper until required.

Repeat until the batter is used up.

To serve, warm the pancakes through in the oven, spoon some Greek yoghurt on top and scatter with blueberries, then pour over a tablespoon of honey.

Pecan and Bourbon Tart

400g sablé pastry
(see page 164)

for the filling:

3 medium eggs

200 g soft brown sugar

270 g golden syrup

pinch of salt

120 ml Bourbon
whiskey

100 g melted unsalted
butter

1 tsp vanilla essence

300 g pecan nuts,
roughly chopped

To make the filling mix all the ingredients, except the pecan nuts, in a food-processor until smooth. Then fold in the pecan nuts and mix well.

To assemble, roll the sablé pastry on a floured table to 5 mm thick.

Grease a large 25-cm tart tin or 8 individual ones.

Line the tins with the pastry, trim the edges and refrigerate for one hour.

Pre-heat the oven to 190°C/gas mark 5.

Fill the tarts with the pecan mixture and bake for about 20–25 minutes until golden.

Serve with vanilla ice cream, crème fraîche or thick double cream.

Bakewell Tart

400 g sablé pastry
(see page 164)

plain flour for dusting

150 g unsalted butter

150 g caster sugar

1 egg, beaten

75 g ground almonds

75 g vanilla sponge
cake, made into crumbs

250 g strawberry jam

30 g flaked almonds

Grease a large 25cm tart tin or 8 individual (8–10 cm) ones.

Roll the sablé pastry on a floured table to 5 mm thick.

Line the tin(s) with the pastry, trim the edges and refrigerate for 1 hour.

Pre-heat the oven to 180°C/gas mark 5.

Cream together the butter and sugar either by hand or in a food-mixer until it is a light creamy colour.

Gradually beat in the egg then fold in the ground almonds and cake crumbs until well mixed.

To assemble the tarts, spread the jam in the bottom of the tart cases, then spoon in the almond mixture to the top.

Smooth it over with a spatula, then scatter the flaked almonds on top.

Bake for about 30–35 minutes until firm to the touch.

Serve with thick custard or double cream.

Caramelised **Rhubarb** with Baked Mascarpone Custard

for the mascarpone custard

150 ml milk

80 ml double cream

80 g mascarpone cheese

1 egg, beaten

7 egg yolks

200 g caster sugar

for the caramelised rhubarb

1 kg rhubarb, trimmed

150 g caster sugar

Pre-heat the oven to 200°C/gas mark 6.

First, make the custard.

Bring the milk and double cream to the boil, add the mascarpone and stir well until it has dissolved. In a bowl whisk together the egg, egg yolks and sugar.

Pour the cream mixture on to the eggs and mix well with a whisk.

Lightly grease 8 ramekins, tea cups or similar-sized heatproof dishes, then fill them with the mixture.

Fill a deep roasting-tin, or similar, with about 2–3 cm of hot water.

Carefully put in the filled cups and bake for 15–20 minutes until the custard has set.

Turn up the oven to 230°C/gas mark 8.

Cut the rhubarb in half lengthways, then cut it into 10-cm lengths.

Heat a roasting-tray or heatproof dish in the oven, then lay in it the pieces of rhubarb and sprinkle over the sugar.

Return to the oven for 15–20 minutes, basting the cooking liquid over the rhubarb every so often.

Remove from the oven and leave to cool a little.

With a spatula, lay the pieces of rhubarb on to plates and spoon some of the cooking syrup over the top.

To remove the mascarpone custards from the pots run the point of a small sharp knife around the edge, invert and turn out on top of the rhubarb.

Rhubarb Crumble

for the rhubarb compote

1 kg rhubarb, cut into 2-cm pieces and washed in cold water

200 g caster sugar

for the crumble topping

200 g soft plain flour

100 g caster sugar

100 g unsalted butter

100 g ground almonds

Pre-heat the oven to 190°C/gas mark 5.

To make the rhubarb compote, put the rhubarb and sugar into a saucepan, cover with a lid and cook gently for 10–15 minutes until the rhubarb softens. Drain in a colander and leave to cool.

to make the crumble topping:

Put all the ingredients into a food-processor and blitz until they resemble fine breadcrumbs.

Put the compote into an ovenproof dish, then scatter over the crumble mixture and bake for 20–25 minutes until golden.

Serve with clotted cream, ice cream or custard.

Elderflower Jelly with Summer Fruits

800 ml water

300 ml Sauternes or a good dessert wine

juice of 1 lemon

400 g caster sugar

40 g leaf gelatine

100 ml elderflower cordial

200 g berries (strawberries, raspberries, blueberries, blackberries etc.)

Bring the water, Sauternes and lemon juice to the boil, add the sugar, stir until it has dissolved then remove from heat.

Soak the gelatine in some cold water for a minute or so until it has softened.

Squeeze out the water, add the gelatine to the syrup and stir until it has dissolved.

Pour in the elderflower cordial, then leave the jelly somewhere cool but do not let it set. Two-thirds fill 8 individual jelly moulds or 1 large one with one half of the berries, then pour in the cooled, but not set, jelly. Leave to set and repeat with the rest of the berries and jelly.

Put the moulds into the fridge for an hour or so to set.

Ricotta and Honey Tart

400 g sablé pastry
(see page 164)

275 g ricotta

275 g mascarpone
cheese

1 tbsp clear honey, plus
extra for serving

1 egg, beaten

Grease a 25-cm tart tin
or 8 individual ones.

Roll the pastry on a
floured table to 5 mm
thick.

Line the tin(s) with it, trim
the edges and refrigerate
for 2–3 hours.

Mix together the ricotta,
mascarpone, honey
and egg and put to one
side.

Pre-heat the oven
to180°C/gas mark 4.

Line the pastry cases
with greaseproof paper,
fill them with baking
beans and bake blind for
10–15 minutes until the
pastry is light golden
round the edges.

Remove the beans and
the paper, then fill the
cases with the ricotta
mixture.

Bake for 10–15 minutes
until the top just starts to
colour.

Serve with good-quality
ice cream, and spoon
over some more honey.

Pannacotta with Raspberries

30 g gelatine

1 vanilla pod, halved
lengthways and seeds
scraped out

300 ml milk

70 g caster sugar

550 ml double cream

300-400 g raspberries

for the raspberry sauce

100 g fresh or frozen
raspberries

30 g caster sugar

Soak the gelatine in cold
water for a few minutes
until soft then squeeze
out the excess water.

Scrape the seeds from
the vanilla pod into the
milk and bring it to the
boil with the sugar and
vanilla pod.

Remove from the heat,
put in the gelatine and
stir until it has dissolved.

Leave to cool, then whisk
in the cream.

Pour into shallow moulds
(6-8 cm ramekins or
similar) and leave to set
in the fridge for 2–3
hours or overnight.

To make the raspberry
sauce, process the
raspberries in a blender
with the sugar and
50 ml water. Strain
through a fine-meshed
sieve.

To serve, dip the moulds
very quickly in and out of
hot water, then turn out
the pannacottas on to
serving plates.

Spoon a little of the
sauce around, then
scatter with raspberries.

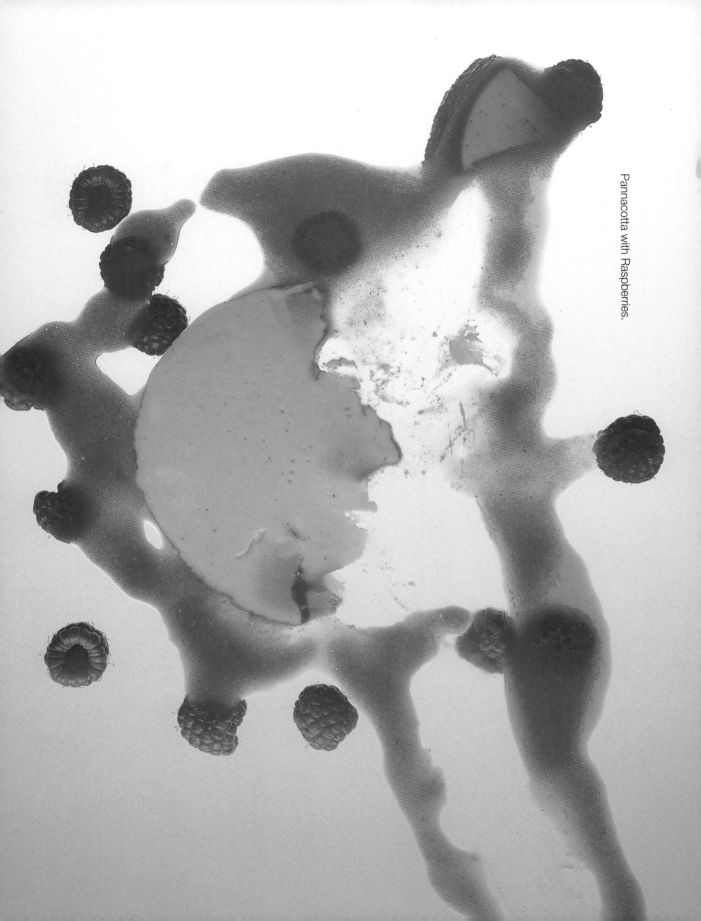

Pannacotta with Raspberries.

An ideal dessert to use up stale brown or white bread.

First seen being served to our staff one day, it was decided to try it in the restaurant with cinnamon ice cream.

300 g water

200 g caster sugar (plus extra for dusting)

$\frac{1}{2}$ tsp ground cinnamon

$\frac{1}{2}$ tsp mixed spice

60 g sultanas

60 g raisins

500 g brown or white bread

4 eggs, beaten

Bread Pudding

Bring the water, sugar, spices, sultanas and raisins to the boil then pour into a large bowl.

Break the bread into small pieces and mix into the dried fruit mix.

Cover with clingfilm and leave to soak overnight.

Pre-heat the oven to 175°C/gas mark 4.

Line a deep baking-tin with greaseproof paper. Fold the eggs into the bread mixture and put it into the baking-tin.

Bake for about 30 minutes until it is firm.

While it is still hot dust the top with caster sugar.

Serve warm with ice cream or clotted cream.

Etiquette

We hadn't really noticed the couple sitting at that table. The girl was, perhaps, prettier than average. Her hair was tied back in a chignon or perhaps a short pony-tail. She hadn't come straight from the office but there was nothing noteworthy about her, not for Le Caprice, not on a Friday night. The room was motoring along happily, the waiters chugged back and forth like tenders. I couldn't have picked out the man she was with from an identity parade of two. Thirty-ish, I suppose, black hair? Brown? Tie? No tie? In retrospect, I assume there wasn't that air of nervous expectation of a first date. He got up to go to the loo, perhaps his getting up was a little emphatic. Did he throw his napkin? I wasn't watching. I was part of my own couple, part of the communal room but not of it, that perfect party that is a full restaurant where you can be in the gang but blissfully only have to talk to the person you came with and the waiter.

When I looked up again, I knew, before seeing, that something was wrong. She was alone at the table, head bent over her wine glass, her hands flat on the cloth. I couldn't see her face but knew that she was crying, silently, deeply. Her shoulders shook with the effort of containing her sobs and then I saw that everyone in the room was aware of her. Like a herd of zebra who'd noticed that one of their number is lame we watched sideways, covertly. A waiter hovered, the *maître d'* and another waiter were having one of those intense corner-of-the-mouth conversations that only serving staff and members of choirs can manage. The hum of civility dropped a gear, faltered, a sudden burst of laughter jarred a false note. Coming to some sort of decision, the girl motioned for the bill, it came express delivery. She drained her glass and head down, shoulders hunched, she left.

The room took a breath and laughed, a vibration of relief ran between the tables. The odd thing was that there had been no drama, no raised voices, no Chablis chucking. In fact every other table in the room was displaying greater histrionics and noisier emotions. Our social antennae were so sensitive that we all knew that something was wrong and it wasn't the Crispy Duck Salad.

Why is a girl we know nothing about, have no connection with, crying? Such a disturbing thing in a restaurant.

Well, the truth is you're not supposed to cry in restaurants. Restaurants aren't built, designed, socially engineered for tears. No one ever advertises a blues bar that's perfectly appointed for sad people who are coming apart at the seams, with quiet corners for contemplating the essential worthlessness of everything, although, heaven knows, there are enough potential customers for one. Dancing naked on the tables in front of your mother-in-law, or inserting your big toe into the fly of your husband's boss is more acceptable behaviour in a restaurant than crying, which on the face of it doesn't make an awful lot of sense, but then, on the face of it, most things about restaurants don't make sense.

We associate public dinner with conversation and honesty and sharing truth, chewing the fat, *in vino veritas*. We ring up a good friend and say I've got to talk to you, can we meet for dinner? We arrange the important verbal, cerebral moments of our life, ones that can't be done over the telephone, where eye contact and epidermal contact are absolutely essential, we arrange them in restaurants, so why is crying so disturbing?

Although restaurants tend not to make sense on the face of it, under their starched linen skin, on a visceral, muscular, blood-and-guts level restaurants make perfect, terrifying sense. They're not about telling it like it is but about telling it like it should be, how we dearly wish it to be. Restaurants are devoted to artifice, we lay the maquillage of manners, etiquette and convention over our animal instincts.

There is more etiquette and manners associated with eating than all other human activities put together. From the earliest age we are taught table manners with a fundamentalist zeal, 'elbows off the table', 'don't talk with your mouth full', 'don't point your knife'. For heaven's sake, how disgusting, other people might be reminded of what it is you're actually doing here. Why do we think the sight of someone eating is so hideous? We all do it. Because it is a bit of our primal, survival-of-the-fittest, miserable origins, hidden in the oldest part of our brains. The bit incidentally that deals with taste and eating is the lizard bit of our brains.

There is a mythology about our beginnings, where we truly come from. Food isn't a polite gavotte of Epicurean taste and mild gluttony. It is life and death, more often death. More of our species have died horribly because of food than anything else, religion, war, the view, race, creed or colour. One or two Tybalts may have succumbed in the name of love, but millions upon millions have come to an end of the coil because of lunch; absence of it, the need for it; defending it; or stealing it is the reason behind most human history. Food is, when all's said and done, the only convertible currency, the only universal standard that really matters, and all of the cold, sweaty, fearful nightmare of our past lurks like a microchip in the back of your head, four inches from those slashing, grinding, foaming teeth. That's why you're not allowed to cry in restaurants.

All the other emotions can be faked, finessed, polished, but tears are the outward and honest sign of unhappiness and unhappiness is first cousin to violence and violence is what we are all trying to forget dinner is really about. We paper and decorate our meals with the bunting of festivity and celebration, we make them special occasions and dress up and save up our most enthusiastic language for food in the hope, against experience, that we will never, ever, ever have to go back to fighting and killing for our survival.

And there is another reason we don't feel comfortable about tears in restaurants. It's that we are vulnerable here. We may feel as safe as a Wiener schnitzel at a vegan convention, but again, that's just on the surface. Underneath, you are a quivering, fearful, children's tea-party jelly. Eating and sleeping are when we are at our most defenceless, sleeping you can lock yourself in, keep a shotgun under the bed, but in public, sat at a table over dinner, you are vulnerable and deep inside we know it.

We tie down meals with endless threads of etiquette like some sleeping Gulliver, as if our animal natures might rear up and smash civilisation back into the prehistoric swamp. Etiquette as opposed to manners. We use the term interchangeably but they are not the same. Manners are putting others at their ease, etiquette is putting everybody in their place. Books on etiquette invariably find their way into the guest loos, good for a laugh, a spot of chuckling ridicule, how absurd these Mrs Manners and a lady-of-breeding persons seem to be. Can people really have cared about these things, these absurd bits of snobbery and pretension? How could anyone take all this rigmarole seriously? But etiquette is deadly serious, with a deadly serious purpose. If you think you are above all that, that you've grown out of all that, that it's all in the past, consider this. Etiquette is the only set of laws that don't have to be made by governments, that don't have to be backed up with a police force, and judges and prisons, and this is because we don't need to be told to make them and because the social retribution for breaking them is all that we need to police them. Etiquette is spread by word of mouth, it is the law of mouth.

You may be thinking that, well, that was right for them back then, when society was rigidly hierarchical and unfair, a time before stress counselling and underpants. When the middle class had every reason to fear the workers and their baser instincts, they might just get it into their heads one night to come with blazing torches and wring the bloated oligarchical necks. If you can keep your position on top of the wheat heap by simply making everyone else insecure about which fork to use then that's brilliant and that would be true if etiquette were carved in stone, if it never changed, if the laws of eating were like the ten commandments. Then you could see them as being the rules of a hierarchical society, but they are not. They change endlessly, elide into new rules. You're never quite sure. It's like learning to do the watusi and discovering that everybody else is doing the twist.

'Eating and sleeping are when we are at our most defenceless, sleeping you can lock yourself in, keep a shotgun under the bed, but in public, sat at a table over dinner, you are vulnerable and deep inside we know it.'

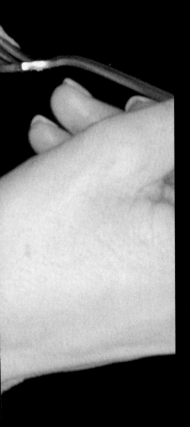

All etiquette seems ridiculous because it invariably makes simple things more difficult and this is on purpose. This is the work of etiquette, to take something that is obvious and make it more complex. I know how to peel an orange, it is obvious, I was born with the equipment to peel oranges, but try doing it without touching it, it's a trick that should get you into the magic circle but then that's etiquette. Passing the port to your left when only the man on your right wants one is ridiculous on the face of it, but only on the face of it.

All the rules are there to be taken advantage of, for instance, we often make difficult or embarrassing decisions in restaurants because the etiquette of the place will protect you from the greater embarrassment of a violent reaction. We fire the office junior in the office because we're not intimidated by them, but you fire a long-term director in a restaurant. We've taken him out of his field of power and, by buying lunch, taken on the power of the restaurant. The unpleasant business can be done with the minimum of fuss, simply because etiquette forbids it. That is why that cad chose Le Caprice to dump the girl who burst into tears. Restaurants are where you start affairs and where you finish them. They are, on the one hand, the very gilded apex of civilisation and, on the other, as close as we ever get to reverting to being animals and that dichotomy is precisely what makes them so wonderfully unique.

Cocktails

Cocktails

How come a Martini is a cocktail but a gin and tonic isn't? Nobody ever asked for a G & T to be shaken not stirred, nor wrote a book on how to make a perfect one, nor bored a bar rigid on the perfect sort of glass for one but in every essential way they are the same. The same number of ingredients, the same level of difficulty, but one is a drink that your eleven-year-old could mix and the other is a cocktail that you need to have a lifetime's experience to even contemplate in your own home. Far safer to let the professionals deal with it. Like the eunuch in charge of the harem used to say, 'this doesn't add up'.

Neither does it make sense. Nothing about cocktails makes sense. Very little about cocktails even tastes like good sense. Cocktails are the triumph of hope over ingredients, fantasy over experience. Before I go on I should say that I don't drink them. I don't drink at all, so you can take my cynicism about cocktails with a pinch of salt. You can dip the whole glass in salt if you like. I didn't drink cocktails when I did drink. They, to the professional, are amateur. They're Friday night, a special occasion, kiddies stuff especially the sweet ones. The addition of sweetness to alcohol shows that you don't take your drinking seriously. Actually there was one cocktail I spent a winter drinking. It's called a Gibson. I drank vodka Gibson which is a martini with a cocktail onion in it. Oddly, and in my case, perceptively, it had been invented by an American ambassador called Gibson who didn't drink and at diplomatic receptions drank soda in a martini glass so that people would think he was joining in. He put an onion in it instead of the olive or a twist so that he didn't sip out of the wrong glass by accident. Everyone assumed it was a martini and the drink was born.

The difference between a drink and a cocktail is the name. Drinks are named by their constituent parts. Cocktails are named like yachts. All cocktails come with an extra ingredient that the barman doesn't put in but that in fact you pay extra for but add yourself. It is the dream of what this little complicated glass is going to do for you or more exactly for your sex life because let's not beat about the bush, cocktails are all about sex. You can use sex to sell anything but the easiest thing to sell with sex is alcohol because sex is so often attained with alcohol.

There is a cocktail that the barmen at Le Caprice mix for me. It's a tall glass filled with half-and-half dry ginger ale and tonic water, a slice of lemon, ice and two drops of Angostura bitters. It hasn't got a name but perhaps an AA would be appropriate.

50 ml of good-quality
vodka or gin

a dash of dry Italian
vermouth

garnish:
a twist of lemon or
two cocktail olives

Variation 1
Dirty Martini

For this variation make as
above, garnish with the
olives and add a half-
teaspoon of juice from
the olive jar.

Variation 2
French Martini

For this variation,
substitute Noilly Prat for
the Italian vermouth.

Garnish with olives
speared on a wooden
cocktail stick.

Variation 3
Gibson

Make as a regular
Martini.

The garnish however
consists of three cocktail
onions speared on to a
wooden cocktail stick.

The Martini

The amount of storage
space you have in your
freezer will determine
which of the two
methods below you will
choose.

If you have space, store
your vodka/gin and the
Martini glasses in the
freezer.

Ensure that you have all
the other ingredients to
hand.

Pour the tiniest drop of
vermouth into each glass
and swirl it around to
coat the inside of the
glass.

Throw any of the
residues out and pour
a generous measure of
gin/vodka into each
glass and garnish with
your choice of lemon
twist or olives.

The Le Caprice method
for making a twist is to
use a cannelet cutter and
cut a continuous strip
(5–10 cm) from around
the lemon while holding it
over the drink.

This releases a generous
spray of lemon oil.

If using olives, spear on a
wooden cocktail stick.

If your chosen spirit is
not frozen, you can
follow this method:

For 'on the rocks' fill a
whisky tumbler full of ice;
for 'straight up' have
your chilled Martini
glasses ready. Into a
mixing glass full of ice,
pour 5 ml of vermouth,
'swirl' or stir gently for
a few seconds to 'coat
the ice' and strain out
any liquid.

Pour in a generous
measure of your
preferred spirit and 'swirl'
again or stir gently for 10
to 15 seconds before
straining into the
prepared glasses.

Sea Breeze

30 ml vodka

cranberry juice

grapefruit juice

for the garnish:

1 orange slice

Fill a 330 ml glass with ice, pour over the vodka and top up with equal amounts of cranberry and grapefruit juice.

Either stir, or tip the contents into a cocktail shaker and back into a glass to mix.

This cocktail works very well if made by the pitcher, but ensure a good supply of ice is kept at hand to refresh your glass.

Pour 150 ml vodka into a litre jug and top up with equal amounts of cranberry and grapefruit

juice until full.
Stir and serve into the ice-filled glasses.

Daiquiri

30 ml white rum

30 ml lemon juice

30 ml sugar syrup

This drink can be served 'on the rocks' in a whisky tumbler or 'straight up' in a Martini-style glass.

Either way, the method is the same.

Fill a cocktail shaker with ice and pour over all the ingredients.

Cover and shake vigorously for 10 seconds and strain into either an ice-filled whisky tumbler or chilled Martini-style glass.

White Lady

30 ml gin

15 ml Cointreau

15 ml lemon juice

Again a cocktail that can be served either 'on the rocks' in a whisky tumbler or 'straight up' in a Martini-style glass.

Either way, the method is the same.

Fill a cocktail shaker with ice and pour over all the ingredients.

Cover and shake vigorously for 10 seconds and strain into either an ice-filled whisky tumbler or chilled Martini-style glass.

Manhattan

The Manhattan has always attracted controversy: should it be dry, sweet or perfect! 'Straight up' or 'on the rocks'? The only answer is to ask for preferences.

30 ml Canadian Club

30 ml Italian vermouth, dry or red (depending upon which type of Manhattan you are making)

2 drops Angostura bitters

for the garnish

lemon twist for a dry Manhattan (made with dry vermouth)

maraschino cherry for a sweet Manhattan (made with red vermouth)

lemon twist/cherry for a perfect Manhattan (made with equal measures of both, totalling 30 ml)

For a Manhattan 'on the rocks', fill a whisky tumbler with ice and pour over the Canadian Club, vermouth and bitters.

Place another inverted tumbler over the first and shake twice. Garnish and serve.

For a Manhattan 'straight up', fill a mixing glass with ice, pour over all the ingredients and stir for 10 seconds.

Strain into a chilled Martini-style glass, garnish and serve.

Pitcher of **Margarita**

This recipe will make 15 servings (a great way to laze away a summer afternoon).

300 ml tequila

300 ml Triple Sec or Cointreau

300 ml lemon juice

Always prepare your glasses first.

If you decide you want a salted rim on your glass, wipe a segment of lemon or lime around the rim, then press it into a saucer of salt and fill with ice.

If you do not require a salt rim simply fill the glasses with ice to the top.

Fill a litre jug with the tequila, Triple Sec or Cointreau and lemon juice.

Stir vigorously for 10 seconds and pour as required into the ice-filled glasses and serve.

If you are only making two Margaritas, use the following method with 30 ml of each of the above ingredients per Margarita.

This method allows you to have the Margarita 'straight up' or 'on the rocks'.

Once again prepare your glasses with salt and ice as described above.

Fill a cocktail shaker with ice, pour over the tequila, Triple Sec or Cointreau and lemon juice.

Cover and shake vigorously for 10 seconds then strain into either an ice-filled whisky tumbler or chilled Martini-style glasses.

Cosmopolitan

50 ml lemon vodka

juice of a lime

measure of Cointreau,
equal to the lime juice

a dash of cranberry

for the garnish:

orange twist

Fill a cocktail-shaker with
ice and pour over all the
ingredients.

Shake for 10 seconds
and strain into a chilled
Martini-style glass.

Garnish with the
orange twist, using
the same method as
for the lemon twist in
Martini (see page 192).

The Bloody Mary is a great favourite at Le Caprice, particularly by the pitcher for Sunday Brunch.

This recipe serves six from a 1-litre jug.

150 ml vodka

60 ml Worcestershire sauce

90 ml lemon juice

18 drops of Tabasco

celery salt to taste

700 ml tomato juice

for the garnish

lime segment for each glass

Pitcher of Bloody Mary

Bloody Mary

Fill your glasses to the top with ice.

Into a 1-litre jug pour the first five ingredients, top up with the tomato juice and stir thoroughly.

Pour into the ice-filled glasses, garnish and serve.

Variations

There are many variations on this classic, many of which involve substituting the vodka with another spirit such as aquavit, for a 'Danish Mary' or with sherry for a 'Spanish Mary'.

The most popular variations, however, involve substituting the tomato juice itself.

Bullshot

Cold tinned beef consommé is used to replace the tomato juice.

Bloody Bull

Use equal amounts of tomato juice and cold tinned beef consommé.

Negroni

20 ml gin

20 ml campari

20 ml red vermouth

soda water (optional)

To serve 'on the rocks' fill a highball glass with ice and pour over all the ingredients, stir, and top up with soda if you wish.

Garnish with an orange twist, using the method as for the lemon twist in Martini (see page 192). If preferred 'straight up' fill a mixing glass with ice and pour over all the ingredients.

Stir for 10 seconds and strain into a chilled Martini-style glass.

No soda is added.

Garnish and serve.

Whisky Sour

25 ml whisky

15 ml lemon juice

15 ml sugar syrup

This drink can be served 'on the rocks' in a whisky tumbler or 'straight up' in a Martini-style glass.

Either way, the method is the same.

Fill a cocktail-shaker with ice and pour over all the ingredients.

Cover and shake vigorously for 10 seconds and strain into either an ice-filled whisky tumbler or chilled Martini-style glass.

Garnish and serve.

Old-fashioned

50 ml Bourbon

1 orange

1 level tsp caster sugar

2 dashes Angostura bitters

1 tsp orange juice

Cut carefully around the skin of the orange with a knife, as you would peel an apple, taking as little of the white pith as possible in one long, continuous piece about 10 cm long and 1.5 cm wide.

Into the bottom of a whisky tumbler put the caster sugar, bitters and the orange juice.
Place the orange peel into the glass so that it snakes its way around the inside.

Using a teaspoon, stir the ingredients so as not to break the orange peel but to dissolve the sugar into the bitters and juice.

Then fill the glass with ice and pour over the Bourbon.

Place another inverted whisky tumbler over the first and shake twice.

Serve.

Old -Fashioned

The Dream

If you ever see a captain of industry, a self-made Goliath, a mover 'n' shaker staring blankly out of the window, chances are he's dreaming of jacking it all in and opening a restaurant or at the very least a bar that serves really good snacks. The reverie of owning your own restaurant is universal and ranges from a banana-leaf hut on a West Indian beach to owning the Ritz.

As a food critic, the most common question I get asked after 'what's the best restaurant in London?' is 'so when are you going to open your own place?' It's a given that any man in possession of a fortune and a few mates wants to stand in a room full of tables wearing a cheesy grin. The question always makes my palms sweat. The very last thing in the whole world I'm either temperamentally or inclined to do is be a restaurateur. As far as I'm concerned it's like asking 'would you rather be lying in a gondola drifting up a canal in Venice with a girl who loved you or be the bloke at the back with a pole and a butcher's hat?' No contest – I know which side of the swing doors I want to be.

Restauranting is one of the toughest, most stressful jobs in the world, the hours are endless and desperately antisocial, the problems are legion and repetitive and mostly the work is grinding, yet still the dream persists. In the Thatcherite 1980s when the redundancy payments were falling thick and fast and 'self-employed' became the most common job description in the country, a huge percentage of all new businesses started up were in catering and ninety per cent of them went bankrupt within two years. Far from being a licence to print luncheon vouchers, catering is most likely to be a quick way to watch your money go up in virgin-olive-oil smoke but still people who should know better stare out of the window and dream of a little seafood place or a rocking, late-night fashion palace ... or a cigar bar or a real French bistro. The restaurant has become the modern Petit Trianon, Marie Antoinette's play farm where she could pretend to be a simple country lass. The restaurant, on the face of it, is very alluring. They're supposed to be a self-contained, simple business – you feed people, they give you money, what you offer is wholly good, it's hospitality and sustenance in a world where everything has got too complex and confused.

Restauranting is a service industry that produces a product but more than that, much more than that, the restaurant is the secular baptistry that contains all the good stuff we want from a modern life. Two hundred years ago it might have been the bucolic romance of a farm, before that perhaps the banker would have dreamt of building a church or monastery for slightly more long-term happiness, today it's a restaurant.

The public dining room is where fashion and sex and business and fame and beauty and entertainment and drama all gavotte. To own all that would be to own a whole slice of civilisation itself, to be a Caesar and Napoleon and Alexander of the menu, to be loved, to be feared and courted, to be phoned up a thousand times a day by people who just wish to sit with you and have fun. A restaurant is a whole semi-detached world where the restaurateur can be a benign despot handing out the largesse of free champagne on the house. You can give access to your world or consign to darkness.

At the end of Bernard Shaw's *Arms and the Man*, the simple but snobbish mother of the Balkan heroine asks the Swiss hero what he is, what he owns. He tells her he has a palace of a thousand rooms and lists all his carriages, his linen, his silver, his hundreds of staff.

'Stop, stop,' she says, 'you must be the King of Switzerland.'
'No, I have the highest title my country can bestow. I'm Mr and I'm a hotelier.'

The dream of owning a restaurant, to be Prospero on your own magic island, to be Rick in your own café is so powerful because nowhere else in our clamorous, high-tension, confused, electric-blink-of-an-eye lives are so many of the contradictory unsolvable Gordian yearnings, urges, imperatives, desires and aspirations collected, correlated so neatly, elegantly, presented on a plate. You have no idea what is actually, truly, on the end of your fork, when you eat at Le Caprice, you couldn't put it in to words, but you can taste it, way back there in the ancient, prehistoric bit of your brain, you can taste it.

Index

A full list of recipes can
be found on page 7

foie gras
Double Fried Egg with
Ceps and **48**

galette
Plum Tomato and
Basil **82**

garlic
Baked Razor Clams
with Parsley and **124**
wild, Parmesan-baked
Marrow with **146**

girolles
Meatloaf with Fried Egg
and **55**

grouse
Roasted **110**

ham
San Daniele, Roasted
Italian Onions with **79**

ham hock
Honey Baked, with
Mustard Sauce **106**
Salad with Puy
Lentils **76**

hash browns
Deep-fried **152**

honey
Honey Baked Ham Hock
with Mustard Sauce **106**
and Ricotta Tart **175**

jelly
Elderflower, with
Summer Fruits **174**

langoustine tails
Fettuccini with **90**

maple syrup
American Pancakes with
168
Potato Pancakes with
Bacon and **52**

marrow
Parmesan-baked, with
Wild Garlic **146**

Martini
Dirty **192**
French **192**
Gibson **192**

muffins
Apricot **47**
Blueberry **47**
Chocolate **47**

mushrooms
Double Fried Egg with
Foie Gras and Ceps **48**
Grilled Field Mushrooms
on French Toast **56**
Meatloaf with Fried Egg
and Girolles **55**
Tagliatelle with Ceps **93**

mustard sauce
Honey Baked Ham Hock
with **106**

onions
Onion and Cider soup,
Creamed **31**
Roasted Italian, with San
Daniele Ham **79**
Tripe and **107**

ox tongue
Cold, and Veal with Baby
Beetroots and Balsamico
105

pancakes
American, with Maple
Syrup **168**
Potato, with Bacon and
Maple Syrup **52**
Ricotta, with Blueberries
and Greek Yoghurt **170**

Parmesan
Parmesan-baked Marrow
with Wild Garlic **146**
waffles, with Baked Plum
Tomatoes and Rocket **54**

parsnip
Soup, Cumin Spiced **30**

partridge
Roasted **110**

pasta
Cannelloni with Peas and
Gorgonzola **91**
Fettuccini with
Langoustine Tails **90**
Tagliatelle with Ceps **93**

pecorino
Risotto with Zucchini
and **86**

pheasant
Roasted **110**

polenta
Grilled Rabbit with
Rosemary, Black Olives
and **116**

potatoes
Crushed, Lobster Salad
with Alsace Bacon and
139
Griddled Scallops with
Mousseline Potato **131**
Potato Pancakes with
Bacon and Maple Syrup
52
Roseval, Truffled, with
Alsace Bacon **74**

puy lentils
Ham Hock Salad with **76**

rabbit
Grilled, with Rosemary,
Polenta and Black Olives
116

raspberries
Pannacotta with **175**

razor clams
Baked, with Parsley and
Garlic **124**

Index